HAWORTH
TIMELINES

Haworth Parsonage © Mark Davis

PAUL CHRYSTAL
WITH PHOTOGRAPHY BY MARK DAVIS

DestinWorld
publishing

ABOUT THE AUTHOR

Paul Chrystal has Classics degrees from the Universities of Hull and Southampton; he worked as a medical publisher for nearly forty years. He is the author of 100 or so books, many of which are about Yorkshire. He is a regular contributor to a number of history magazines, is a reviewer for 'Classics for All', he writes for a national daily newspaper, and has appeared on the BBC World Service, Radio 4's PM programme and various BBC local radio stations in York, Manchester, Cleveland and Sheffield. See www.paulchrystal.com.

Mark Davis is a professional photographer and author. He specialises in architecture, landscape, show home, property and location portraiture. See www.mark-davis-photography.com

First published 2018
Destinworld Publishing Ltd
www.destinworld.com

British Library Cataloguing in Publication Data.
A catalogue record for this book is available from the British Library.

ISBN 978 1 9997175 1 3

Cover design by John Wright

BY THE SAME AUTHOR

Yorkshire Literary Landscapes

Historic England: Bradford

Old Saltaire & Shipley

Bradford at Work

Pubs In & Around York

The Place Names of Yorkshire – Including Yorkshire Pub Names

Leeds in 50 Buildings

The Confectionery Industry in Yorkshire

Yorkshire Murders, Manslaughter, Madness & Executions, in press

For a full list please visit www. paul.chrystal.com

ACKNOWLEDGEMENTS

The book has been immeasurably improved by the generosity of a number of Haworth people. They include Mark Davis whose stunning photography graces many of the pages; Rosie Wright, Business Development Manager, Wyedean; Simon Packham, And Chocolate Ltd; Haworth Ukulele Group; Margaret Silver and Simon Palmer for permission to use the Simon Palmer watercolour published in Jim Greenhalf's *Salt & Silver*.

The Black Bull. © Mark Davis

The graveyard. © Mark Davis

CONTENTS

INTRODUCTION

Haworth expresses the Brontës; the Brontës express Haworth; they fit like a snail to its shell.

[Virginia Woolf, 1904]

The Brontë sisters.
From left to right, they are Anne, Emily and Charlotte; Branwell originally painted himself between Emily and Charlotte, but later painted himself out. Circa 1834/National Portrait Gallery: NPG 1725

The old white Black Bull. © Mark Davis

Haworth Moor. © Mark Davis

Main Street. © Mark Davis

This book is about Haworth, a former industrial village 800 feet up on the blasted moors south of Keighley. Until the modern tourist boom it was a wretched one-horse village where the busiest place was the graveyard, overflowing and leeching its rainwater and snow melt into the local water supply, lethally filtered through the decomposing corpses of the Haworth deceased. Until Patrick Brontë's valiant efforts and the damning Babbage Report, sewage was a common sight and smell as it swilled its way down Main Street; this, and the absence of domestic sanitation and desperate overcrowding, made it a place that vied with industrial Bradford and London's East End as a fetid, polluted hell on earth up to and including the time when the Brontës made their home here in the parsonage at the top of the hill.

The cramped houses hummed with the industry of textile workers until the mills down the hill with their newfangled machines discarded many of the men, choosing instead to work the women and children half to death on profit-raising lower rates of pay.

The Brontës are, and will for ever be, umbilically joined to Haworth. In one respect the Brontës changed everything; in another, socially and industrially, sanitation apart, things remained much the same despite the international fame and celebrity the sisters and their wayward brother brought to the village. The Brontë sisters remained aloof from their fellow villagers and chose instead to escape to the wuthering and wasted moors above Haworth – the essence of and inspiration for their wonderful novels and poetry. The change they did effect was, of course, the global tourism their work attracted, making Haworth a literary magnet, a place of pilgrimage for the world's literati and dilettante, and for the plain curious.

Today, that interest persists and grows by the year. Today, Haworth is a pleasing, neat and rewarding place to visit with a reputation for culture and entertainment. Main Street is a bright and buzzing hill. The Parsonage Museum is model of preservation and restoration, and a shining beacon on our national literary heritage, up there with the Lake District and Hardy's Wessex.

Haworth Timeline attempts to show the stark dichotomy between the former industrial and polluted village with its manifest social problems and, largely through Mark Davis' stunning photography, the picturesque place of twenty-first-century literary pilgrimage, 800 feet up on the wuthering moors.

Paul Chrystal
Yorkshire, May 2018

All Saints and All Angels'. © Mark Davis

The parsonage. © Mark Davis

Ponden Moor. © Mark Davis

Haworth graveyard. © Mark Davis

HAWORTH BEFORE THE BRONTËS

Haworth, situated on the eastern slope of the Pennines near to the river Worth, comes alive relatively late in our island's history. The Romans left their mark in the vicinity with a road that is thought to have passed near Manywell Heights, and the name Stanburgh (on the road to Colne, the 'Colony' of the Romans,) suggests a fortification. There was nothing there in William I's 1086 *Domesday Book*, which recorded landholdings before and after his conquest.

Etymologically speaking the name Haworth means a 'hedged or hawthorn enclosure'; a 1771 map has it as 'Howorth', a misspelling. Haworth is notorious for the steep climb that is Main Street: at the top the mark on the church reveals that it is 796.1 feet above sea level; down in the valley opposite the railway station near the Royal Oak pub another mark gives an elevation of 556.4 feet, 240 feet lower. The two marks are half a mile apart, which accounts for the, at times, 1 in 10 gradient.

Main Street in snow, February 27 2018. © Mark Davis

Trudging up that steepest of hills in 2011. © Mark Davis

The first precise record comes as late as 1296 when we hear of it as 'a settlement' in the 'Kirkby's Inquest', when Godfrey de Haworth, Roger de Manyngham, and Alicia de Bercroft, had four oxgangs in Haworth. William de Horton had four oxgangs in Oxenhope, and William de Clayton held another four oxgangs in Oxenhope.

An oxgang was the amount of land tillable by one ox in a ploughing season, typically about fifteen acres; a virgate was the amount of land tillable by two oxen in a ploughing season; a carucate was the land tillable by a team of eight oxen in a ploughing season.

Nostell Priory held lands in Oxenhope in the thirteenth century: 'Richard de Haworth had a dispute with the Prior of Nostell respecting certain lands and a warren between Oxenhope and Haworth which was settled by agreement.' In 1311, on the death of the Earl of Lincoln, an inquisition was carried out, which shows that the Haworths held land in Haworth at that time.

The *Nomina Villarum* of 1316 records Haworth and Oxenhope as owned by Nicholas de Audley, who held Bradford Manor. Richard II's poll tax of 1380 lists forty persons as inhabitants of Haworth, each of whom paid the tax of four pence. Bradford township, by comparison, had fifty-nine persons charged. *Barnard's Survey*, taken in 1577, gives us the following:

> In Haworth was a carucate of land, formerly in the possession of John Haworth, afterwards of Roger de Manningham and John de Bercroft, lately of John Rishworth, and now of Alexander Rishworth, held by service as the eighth part of a knight's fee; in which town the said Alexander claims to hold the manor by reason of the said land. Similarly, under Oxenhope, the Eltofts claimed the manor.

Haworth from above. © Mark Davis

The last will of William Horsfall, of Haworth, made on 1 July 1536, makes interesting reading, showing the importance and value of 'the household stuffe':

> To the church he gave – , to the curate –. To Thomas his son xls. To Richard his son – . To Margaret his daughter a 'cowe'. To William his son, a bedde of clothes. The reversion of the household stuffe to Margaret and Elizabeth his daughters. To Margaret daughter of his son Thomas ... To Richard Horsfall my beste iackett, my beste doblet and my beste hose.

As indeed does the will of Mary, daughter of Richard Sunderland, of High Sunderland, 1574, who gave:

> (inter alia) to Abraham, son of Henry Rishworth 2s., to Robert son of John Rishworth 3s. 4d., To the wyfe of John Ryshworth of laynehead, Haworth 20s., to Christopher Ryshworth 20s., to Anne his syster, 10s., to Henry Rishworth 10s., to Jennet daughter of John Rishworth 10s., to John Rishworth, wolman, of Boothes town [near Halifax] 10., to the wyfe of John Rishworth one reade gathered pettycote, a paire of black sieves and one rayment of lynnen. To Jennet my sister and to the wyffe of John Rishworththe rest of my rayment.

The legacies of the local landed gentry were, of course, significantly more lucrative, as this will made out in 1540 for Sir John Halifax clearly shows:

> SIR JOHN HALIFAX, of the parish of Haworth, seke in bodie, gave his soul to our ladie, and his bodie to be buried at St. Michael's. To Mr. George Gargrave my Jacket; to Margaret my sister, my horse; to Edward Akerode my gown; to William Allerton myne olde gowue; to Richard Akerode towc dubletts, a mattres, and three sheits, a saddle and a bridell; to Grace Ackerode, towe courletts, two shets and a blanket; to Thomas Lister a paire of hosse clothe; to Henry Ackerode a cloke, and to Anne, his wife, a silver spone; to Sir John of Watterhouse my bonnett; to Henry Ackerode my hatte; to Henry Scladen a paire of hose; to Robert Waddsworth a paire of hose; to Sir Thomas Hall towe books; to Sir Steven Smyth towe books; to Henry Ackerode the rest of my books.

Taxation returns in 1545 tell us that there were seventy-three households; if we assume an average 4.5 people per family, we get a population of around 300, up from half that in 1379. By 1643 that had risen to 650, if the Fairfax Ley is anything to go by. In 1662, 490 Haworth people over sixteen paid the poll tax, giving a population of 700 or so.

The Registers at Haworth for the seventeenth century show the weather to be unpredictable, and astrology to be alive and well:

> On the 17th July, 1646, there is an entry recording a great tempest, with thunder and lightnings, such as few have heard or seen. In 1648, a great fall of snow on Fastens Even which continued till the last week of the same winter. February 25th, 1649, two suns appeared on either side of the

true sun, making three in all. 1652: such a drought between and the first week in June that during that season, only one shower. Notwithstanding there was a good harvest. August 20th, there was a storm of wind and hail, some shaped like spur rowels. It was the effect of the conjunction of Saturn and Mars in Leo. There were two crops of bilberries.

Bad weather, of course, made life difficult and had an impact on harvests; the 1644 and 1648 summers were very wet; there were droughts in 1652 and 1657 while 1658 was very wet.

In 1660, the number of persons assessed by the Poll Act within Haworth Constabulary was 490, which included all the inhabitants over fifteen years of age, except a few paupers. The amount of the tax was £35, and the total rent of the lands and mills was £1,020. There were twenty-six baptisms, three marriages and eight burials; the population was around 700. In 1664, eight persons were sent to Halifax Corrections, and afterwards excommunicated for non-appearance: seven men for not coming to church, and a woman for fornication.

The 1666 Hearth Tax reveals 158 households in Haworth, 122 of which (77 per cent) paid for one hearth, twenty-five (14 per cent) for two hearths and eleven for three or more. As might be expected, this tells us that the majority of the housing stock was small and modest.

Haworth's population grew rapidly during the first half of the eighteenth century, from 800 in 1702. The village lacked a sewage system and the well water was polluted by faecal matter and the decomposition of bodies in the cemetery up the hill. This, of course, had serious health and hygiene consequences: life expectancy was less than 25 years and infant mortality was around 41 per cent of children under six months of age.

Most of the people in an around Haworth worked on the unyielding land on the moors and supplemented their incomes with work done at home, such as spinning and weaving wool shorn from the sheep that were farmed on the moors. At this time, ten spinners were required to supply the yarn to keep one full time weaver busy.

By 1740 worsted production was evident throughout Haworth, but towards the end of the century cotton was important and should not be forgotten, with mills, for example, in Ponden and Mytholm, Royd House and Bridgehouse Mill.

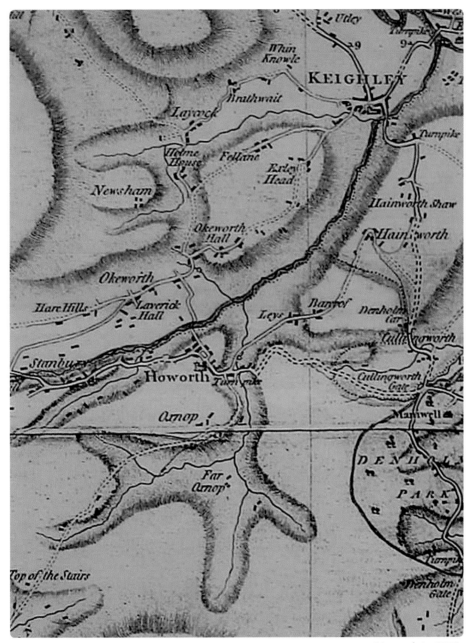

Haworth in 1771.

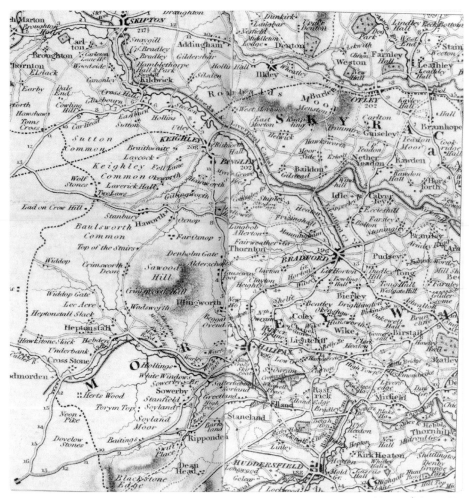

Haworth in 1822.

But it was wool that prevailed. After 1800, with the invention of the false reed or slay, there was a major economic change: this was due to the introduction of labour-saving machinery, particularly wool combing machines, in the mills constructed on the banks of the River Worth, and on the Bridgehouse and Oxenhope Becks whose waters turned the mill wheels. This provided employment for many Haworth women and children but, increasingly, fewer Haworth men were called on to work the machines and produce the textiles; many of the male workers crossed over to Bridgehouse Beck to the Brow or commuted to other towns for work.

Nevertheless, about one-third of the 3,164 Haworth inhabitants – men, women, and children – in the Brontës' day would have worked in the ten state-of-the-art mills in Haworth and the surrounding villages busy turning out worsted yarns for the lucrative export markets.

HAWORTH IN THE NINETEENTH CENTURY

Not unnaturally, many people assume the Haworth of the Brontë era to be a neat, picture- postcard moorland village. It was, of course, nothing of the sort. It may surprise some to know that the village of Haworth and the surrounding villages were predominantly industrialised, not an impression easily obtained from the picture we get from descriptions in *Wuthering Heights*. Then, it was an overcrowded industrial town: polluted, stinking and lethally unhealthy. The death rate was just as high as London's or Bradford's, with 41.6 per cent of children never making their sixth birthday. The average age at death was just 25.8.

To put this into some context, Bradford was one of the most polluted towns in England in the nineteenth century: sewage routinely flowed into Bradford Canal (the 'River Stink') and Bradford Beck (the principal source of drinking water from the river), causing outbreaks of cholera and typhoid. A mere 30 per cent of children born to wool combers lived to see the age of fifteen. Life expectancy at eighteen years was one of the country's lowest.

Between 1843 and 1846, George Weerth, the German writer friend of Marx and Engels, in between researching the impact of the Industrial Revolution on the relationship between property owner and the workers, worked in Bradford as a representative for a textile firm. In 1846 he described the town in *Neue Rheinische Zeitung* as follows:

> Every other factory town in England is a paradise in comparison to this hole. In Manchester the air lies like lead upon you; in Birmingham it is just as if you were sitting with your nose in a stove pipe; in Leeds you have to cough with the dust and the stink as if you had swallowed a pound of Cayenne pepper in one go – but you can put up with all that. In Bradford, however, you think you have been lodged with the devil incarnate. If anyone wants to feel how a poor sinner is tormented in Purgatory, let him travel to Bradford.

From the start of the nineteenth century the population in and around Haworth started to boom: in 1801, 3,164 people lived in the township; in 1811, there were 3,971; in 1821, there were 4,668; in 1831, there were 5,835. In 1841 Haworth had 2,434, Far Oxenhope 1,910, Near Oxenhope 1,013, and Stanbury 946, giving a total population for the parish of 6,303. In 1871 Haworth had 2,700, Far Oxenhope 1,704, Near Oxenhope 808, and Stanbury 754; a total of 5,966 – a decrease of 300 from 1841, but an increase of nearly 3,000 on 1801 (59.66 per cent).

The Brontës arrived on 25 February 1820 from Thornton near Bradford at what Elizabeth Gaskell in her *Life of Charlotte Brontë* describes as 'a lawless, yet not unkindly population' [p. 31]; the sisters tell us little about the village, a place in which they did not integrate but remained socially aloof. In 1835, Patrick Brontë was equally stand-offish when he asserts that, while civil at all times, 'I have not tried to make any friends, nor have I met with any whose mind was congenial with my own'.

In 1845, Charlotte's experience of the place allowed her to chime in with:

> [Haworth is a place] where education had made little progress and where consequently there was little inducement to seek social intercourse beyond our own domestic circle, we were wholly dependent on ourselves and on each other, on books, and study, for enjoyments and occupations of life.

So, cocooned and insulated by their lives in the parsonage, the sisters got on with writing their books as if Haworth and the people of Haworth did not exist. They do, of course, say much more about the village's moorland environs through their novels and poetry.

Who would come out anyway in weather like this? © Mark Davis

Indeed, we have to wait until 1850 for the first detailed account of Haworth the village, offered as background information by Gaskell in her biography of Charlotte Brontë in 1857 – an invaluable source of information about Haworth. Her biography begins with introductory chapters, the first of which is her description of the surrounding countryside and of Haworth itself, the parsonage and the church with its extensive burial ground. She observes that the four miles between Keighley and Haworth were peppered with:

> Villas, great worsted factories, rows of workmen's houses, with here and there an old-fashioned farmhouse and outbuildings, it can hardly be called 'country' any part of the way … the air is dim and lightless with the smoke from all these habitations and places of business.

The road to Haworth. © Mark Davis

And then Haworth itself appears:

> Right before the traveller on this road rises Haworth village; he can
> see it for two miles before he arrives, for it is situated on the side of
> a pretty steep hill, with a background of dun and purple moors, rising
> and sweeping away yet higher than the church, which is built at the
> very summit of the long narrow street. All round the horizon there is
> this same line of sinuous wave-like hills; the scoops into which they fall
> only revealing other hills beyond, of similar colour and shape, crowned
> with wild, bleak moors – grand, from the ideas of solitude and loneliness
> which they suggest, or oppressive from the feeling which they give of
> being pent-up by some monotonous and illimitable barrier, according to
> the mood of mind in which the spectator may be.

[pp. 12–13]

Haworth in the distance.

On reaching the village, Gaskell observed:

> The ascent through the village begins … The old stone houses are high compared with the width of the street, which makes an abrupt turn before reaching the more level ground at the head of the village, so that the steep aspect of the place in one part is almost like that of a wall.

Main Street in 2011. © Mark Davis

Her journey ends with the first glimpse of the church and, her destination, the parsonage:

> They pass into the quiet little by-street that leads to Haworth Parsonage. The churchyard is on one side of this lane, the school-house and the sexton's dwelling (were the curates formerly lodged) on the other.

The parsonage at last. © Mark Davis

Gaskell found qualities of 'independence' and 'self-sufficiency' with a 'strong sagacity' and 'dogged power of will' in the Yorkshire folk she encountered; they were somewhat off-putting to a stranger [p. 17]. The people of Haworth were 'wild, rough. Their accost is curt; their accent and tone of speech blunt and harsh'. To Gaskell, soon to be well-schooled in squalor and poverty through the research she did for her social novel, *Mary Barton* (1848) investigating the Manchester poor between 1839 and 1842, what she found that day in Haworth would have neither shocked nor surprised. She is under no illusion about the privations inflicted on local populations by the 'mixture of agricultural with manufacturing that ensued and prevailed'. She knew all too well that the romantic, bucolic image of country life, 'the vision of pastoral innocence' had no place in anti-idyll Haworth. The vocabulary she uses to describe the firsthand reports gleaned from the locals includes words and phrases such as 'coarseness', 'unncouthness of the rustic', 'the sharpness of the tradesman', and 'irregularity and fierce lawlessness'. In many respects the Brontës were immune to all of this: they were never well off but they were comfortable; they were highly literate and educated; their father commanded respect in the community and they were cocooned within and isolated in the parsonage on the hill. If school-teaching next door is excluded, only Branwell and Patrick Brontë really engaged in community village life in any meaningful way: the one secular, the other religious.

Gaskell tells it how it was [pp. 95–96]:

> The village is built with an utter disregard of all sanitary conditions. The great old churchyard lies above the houses, and it is terrible to think how the very water-springs of the pumps below must be poisoned. But this winter of 1833–4 was particularly wet and rainy, and there was an unusual number of deaths in the village. A dreary season it was to the family in the parsonage: their usual walks obstructed by the spongy state

of the moors the passing and funeral bells so frequently tolling, and filling the heavy air with their mournful sound, and, when they were still, the 'chip, chip', of the mason, as he cut the gravestones in a shed close by.

Charlotte Brontë primed Gaskell well when she wrote to her in this uncompromising letter:

> When you come to Haworth, you must do it in the spirit which might sustain you in case you were setting out on a brief trip to the back woods of America. Leaving behind your husband, children and civilisation, you must come out to barbarism, loneliness and liberty.

Her father had been no less forgiving in this letter of 4 August 1843 to the National Society regarding the Haworth Sunday School:

> I have resided in Yorkshire above thirty years, and have preached and visited in different parishes … the populace in general are either ignorant or wicked, and in most cases where they have a little learning it is of a schismatical, vainly philosophical or treacherously political nature.

However, Gaskell, like us, finds the ubiquity of death in Haworth quite remarkable, with villagers rubbing shoulders on a daily basis with the reaper, and the oversubscribed graveyard in a commanding position at the top of the village a constant reminder of the inevitability of death sooner rather than later. This familiarity inculcated a stoical indifference to death and all its paraphernalia; the terrible death toll within the Brontë family was not unusual and would have left little impression on the village population. Patrick Brontë and Nicholls officiated at more than 1,300 burials in ten years, which tells us that 25 per cent of the population was dying every ten years, a death toll sustained by an average steady population growth.

Charlotte's ghostly 'tombstones grey'. © Mark Davis

The funereal landscape outside the front door certainly had an impact on Emily Brontë as these opening lines from the sombre *I See Around Me Tombstones Grey* show:

> I see around me tombstones grey
> Stretching their shadows far away.
> Beneath the turf my footsteps tread
> Lie low and lone the silent dead –
> Beneath the turf – beneath the mould –
> Forever dark, forever cold –
> And my eyes cannot hold the tears
> That memory hoards from vanished years
> For Time and Death and Mortal pain
> Give wounds that will not heal again …
> Sweet land of light! thy children fair
> Know nought akin to our despair –
> Nor have they felt, nor can they tell
> What tenants haunt each mortal cell,
> What gloomy guests we hold within –
> Torments and madness, tears and sin!

In his 1879 *Haworth, Past and Present: A History of Haworth, Stanbury and Oxenhope*, J.H. Turner gives a description of relative isolation:

> Embosomed in the high moorlands connected with the Pennine Range, is the ancient village of Haworth, with the hamlets of Stanbury and Oxenhope in its township. The ancient chapelry comprises an area of 10,540 acres, stretching from the village of Haworth (four miles south-west of Keighley,) westward to the boundary of Lancashire, nearly half of which is uncultivated moors, heaths and commons. The township is in the parish of Bradford, yet completely isolated from the rest of that parish, being eleven miles distant from the town. Before the Worth Valley Railway was opened it was a point of some difficulty to decide upon the best means of reaching this ancient village.
>
> [pp. 9–10]

Manesseh Hollindrake's draper's shop at 111 Main Street in the 1890s. Manessah also farmed; his son James was a butcher at no 66. Mrs Hollindrake, probably, at the door.

Haworth was more commercially important than the neighbouring settlements because the important trans-Pennine Bluebell Turnpike from west of Bradford to east of Colne ran down Main Street; the village also served an expansive rural hinterland which relied on the village. There was a toll in Main Street that benefitted from the traffic in lime, and other commodities. In 1841 the Brontës would have seen in their village at one time or another at least forty-four tradesmen and sixty types of artisans, including: stationers; booksellers; fifteen grocers; five butchers and four bakers; drapers, a clockmaker and surgeons. On the social side there were six innkeepers, spirit merchants or sellers of beer. These were complemented by twenty shoemakers, ten tailors, six makers of dresses and seven blacksmiths; two clockmakers and a barber. All of this added up to a buzzing little village where most of the essentials of life could be had on the doorstep. By 1851 the local commercial activity had grow to ninety tradesman and ninety artisans so it was undoubtedly on the up. A post office opened in 1843. By 1861, the numbers increased to 105 and 103 despite a fall in population of 1,000.

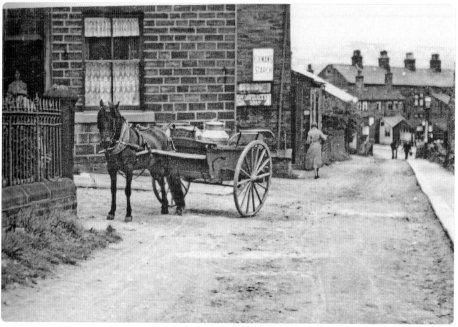

The milkman in Cold Street with the fish and chip shop and the pie and peas shop in Sun Street in the background.

A Snowy King's Arms and Olde White Lion, 27 February 2018. © Mark Davis

The Olde White Lion. © Mark Davis

Clustered around the square at the foot of the church steps – essentially the village centre – were an apothecary, a wine and spirit merchant, stationers, an ironmonger-cum- postmaster, a temperance hotel and four inns: the Black Bull, the Old White Lion, the Cross, and the King's Arms.

The paper shop in Main Street in 1963; he was also at 111 after Hollindrake's closed. It later became a second hand bookshop. The building to the left, later a café, was the old Liberal Club.

The square with the Brontë Café/woods sweet shop on the right
and the Yorkshire Penny Bank in the background.

The village could also boast a Cooperative Society with its shop, originally in the central square but from 1897 further down Main Street, 'Haworth Industrial Cooperative Society Limited Central Stores'; it originally provided drapers', butchers' and grocers' departments on the ground floor and an 'assembly room' on the top floor.

There was also a branch of the Yorkshire Penny Bank, which opened in 1860 but by 1894 had moved with its grand turret to what is now the Visitor Information Centre.

These staple businesses were joined by the usual trades, including boot and clog makers, a blacksmith and joiners, plasterers and stone masons. A typical description of everyday life in the village comes from a visitor staying at the Black Bull who was:

> just looking from the window which gave on the square. Indifferent to the rain, the people clattered by in their wooden shoes. Two toddlers, bare necked and bare armed, stood hand-in-hand, looking wistfully into the window of a bake shop, where a tempting array of loaves round and square, of tea cakes and currant buns and seed and plum cakes, riveted their gaze. The vicar passed by with the Curate in earnest conversation … a huge cart horse struggled upward with a heavy load, slipping backward almost every step of the steep way, while the carter in dingy smock walked at his head and sought to ease and encourage his beast. Grimy mill hands passed, taciturn and grave; a man with a squealing pig had difficulties in driving the porker, who bolted into every lane and doorway … the draper next door came to his window to watch the pig's divagations [wandering away].

The Black Bull. © Mark Davis

An early view of an earlier telephone box.

When Patrick Brontë arrived he inherited a parish blighted by unemployment. Haworth men typically had two jobs if they were to make ends meet. On the one hand, they were subsistence farmers, working a few unyielding acres on the moors, which they combined with handloom weaving or wool-combing, selling their wares in markets such as Halifax and York. The peat they dug was Haworth's main fuel. Others doubled up as butchers, carters or clog makers. However, the microeconomics of Haworth were on the cusp of major change: the recently ubiquitous cottage worsted weaving on a loom in front rooms or upstairs was already in serious decline when the Brontë family arrived in the village in 1820. New water-powered mills had been springing up along the River Worth from 1790, and the local economy began its inexorable drift from the domestic to the industrial.

Agriculture and textiles apart, the area supported millstone grit quarrying, especially on Nab Hill where fifteen quarrying firms gave work to 300 men and fifty horses in 1560 to satisfy the demand for housing boom building materials in the growing cities, towns and villages. There was a limited amount of mining too on what was the northern seam of the Yorkshire coalfield on Penistone Hill. Other seams yielded low grade coal at Sawood, Far Oxenhope and Stanbury Moor.

Food was relatively scarce, often little more than gruel or porridge, resulting in widespread vitamin deficiency. As noted, public hygiene was atrocious: lavatories were crude. The facilities at the parsonage were no more than a plank across a hole in a hut at the rear, with a lower plank for the children. Dental health was little in evidence: Charlotte Brontë, for example, was described in her thirties as having a toothless jaw by Elizabeth Gaskell, who wrote in a letter dated 25 August 1850 to Catherine Winkworth: that she had 'a large mouth and many teeth gone'.

The main industry had moved out of the cottages into the factories for the large-scale production of worsted yarn and cloth; the biggest factory in Haworth was Bridgehouse Mills on the Bridgehouse Beck in the valley below the village. The 1851 census reveals what you would expect – many households had fathers, mothers, sons and daughters employed in the textile industry. A good example is sixty-year-old John Mitchell and his wife, of Hall Green: they worked as handloom weavers, a vanishing occupation by that time with looms set up in their cottage. Their two daughters, however, worked as power loom weavers in one of the local mills. Their son was a wool comber, which involved combing raw wool to produce fibres ready for spinning; this was still done in the houses of the workers and was a hard and dangerous occupation because of the charcoal or coal stoves to heat the combs, and stoves that were rarely allowed to go out so the fumes caused illness and death because windows were rarely opened.

The cottages in Haworth were typically built of local sandstone and gritstone, with dressed stone surrounds to the doorways and characteristically Pennine mullioned windows. Some were back-to-back and some had a dank and dingy cellar dwelling below. More impressive housing included the seventeenth-century Old Hall at Hall Green; on North Street there is another fine seventeenth-century house with an aisled barn adjacent to Townend Farm. The parsonage was built in 1779 and has a symmetrical elevation and sash windows, rather than the mullioned windows of the cottages; Woodlands, the home of the family that ran Bridgehouse Mills, has a splendid classical front.

The village saw considerable expansion after the opening of the Keighley and Worth Valley Railway in 1867; at the same time, many of the local mills mushroomed into large steam-powered factories. The timing for the railway could not have been better, for it was around this time that Brontë-led tourism really exploded in the area – what better way now to get (most of the way) to Haworth than by steam train?

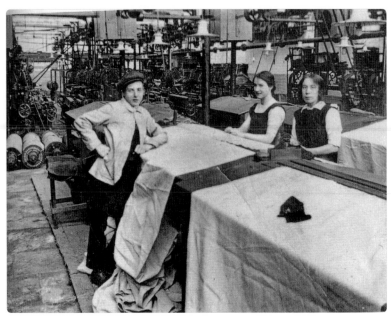

A mill hand, two burlers and menders posing in Rushworth Lund's worsted mill in North Street around 1930. The looms are in the background.

Townend Farm, about 1900 just behind the Rushworth Lund mill; the building on the right belonged to the mill. Willie Binns, the farmer in the early twentieth century, was also a carrier; his cart is in the foreground.

Haworth health and disease

Admittedly, the clear, clean air and crystal becks of the moors were not very far from the village, but it was in the village that the people had to live, and die. In 1850, a searching government investigation by Benjamin Herschel Babbage revealed Haworth as dirty, unhygienic, and with shockingly high mortality rates that could compete with the country's worst. Babbage's research was instigated by Patrick Brontë who, as parish curate, was only too aware of the carnage wreaked by the insanitary conditions endured by his parishioners on and down the hill.

The findings of Babbage's report are nothing short of shocking. The skyline of this small industrial mill town was punctuated by tall chimneys belching out toxic smoke. The British Library website on the report gives a summary that tells us how:

> Excrement ran down the street; for want of sewers, fenced in areas held human waste, offal from the slaughterhouse and pigsty waste for up to months at a time. Housing was poorly ventilated and overcrowded, with several dwellings in cellars. Perhaps most appallingly, Babbage's investigation confirmed that the graveyard, situated on the hill at the top of the town and in front of the Brontës' home, was so overcrowded and poorly oxygenated that decomposing, putrid matter filtered into the water supply. … there was a chronic shortage of privies with only one for every four or five families.
>
> [www.bl.uk/collection-items/sanitary-report-on-haworth-home-to-the-bronts]

It is worth quoting extracts from the report in order to get the detail in all its unpleasantness; the squalor here was surely as bad as anywhere at the time. On sewerage:

> There are no water closets in the town, and only 69 privies, being little more than one privy to every four and a half houses. … I found seven houses in the main street without a privy. … I found twenty four houses lower down with only one privy amongst them. … I believe that it would be found that there are no more than two dozen houses in the whole town that have a privy to themselves. … two of the privies used by two dozen each, are in the public street, not only within view of the houses, but exposed to the gaze of passers by, whilst a third, as though even such a situation were too private, is perched upon an eminence commanding the whole length of the street. The cesspit of this privy lies below it, and opens by a small door into the main street; occasionally this door is burst open by the superincumbent weight of night soil and ashes, and they overflow into the public street, and at all times a disgusting effluvium escapes through this door into the street. Within two yards of this cesspit door there is a tap for the supply of water to the neighbouring houses … there are no sewers in Haworth; … as a consequence of the want of sewerage there is a contiguous to each privy a receptacle for the night soil, in some cases walled round … into these midden-steads are thrown the household refuse and the offal from the slaughter-houses, where mixed with the night soil and occasionally with the drainage from

pigsties, the whole lies exposed for months together, decomposition goes on and the offensive smells and putrid gases are given off in close proximity to dwelling-houses, making them much more injurious.

Old Haworth

With regards water supply, only thirty to forty houses enjoyed the luxury of clean running water. Landowners ensured that locals had no access to local springs. Most of the villagers were obliged to take a chance on water from two wells: the Head Well, and Brigg Well at the bottom of Main Street.

perhaps the most crying want of Haworth is water, of which there is an absolute dearth in the dry season ... very few of the inhabitants use the pump-water for cooking or drinking, as they do not fancy that the water is pure and when the soakage into the ground from the midden-stead, and the small depth of the pump-wells are considered, there appears every reason to suppose that the general opinion upon this subject is correct ... the supply of water upon the Head Well is so scant in the summer time that in order to have water for the Monday's washing, the poor people are in the habit of going there at 2 or 3 o'clock on Monday morning, in order to wait their turn to fill their cans and buckets from the slowly running stream. It is stated that the water at this well is very bad at this season, and it is sometimes so green and putrid that cattle, which have been driven there to drink, after tasting the water, have turned away and refused to touch it again.

[Public Health Act (11 & 12 Vict., cap. 63.) Report ... on a preliminary inquiry into the sewerage, drainage, and supply of water, and the sanitary condition of the inhabitants of the hamlet of Haworth (1850)]

Babbage identified pockets of chronic overcrowding: one in the triangle formed by West Lane, North Street and Ginnel (today's Changegate); the other Gauger's Croft (where the Medical Centre is now). The Croft was home to a wine warehouse, a timber yard, a pauper, a Chelsea pensioner; of the remaining twenty-nine, eighteen were wool-combers all living with a suffocating and fetid occupancy of 5.2 people per bijoux house – some of which were nothing more than cellars prone to flooding.

Gauger's Croft in 2013. © Mark Davis

Dirty water apart, the usual culprits had a lethal hand in debilitating or carrying away the dead: Patrick Brontë died from bronchitis; five of his six children died from TB; sexton John Brown died aged twenty-eight from 'dust on the lungs' (pneumoconiosis); typhus fever and diarrhoea were rife; cholera paid visits in 1842 and 1849. The parsonage copy of *Graham's Modern Domestic Medicine* is heavily annotated in Patrick Brontë's hand.

Presented to the General Board of Health, the report successfully prompted work to improve the town's parlous sanitation through the establishment of a Local Board of Health – despite vigorous and venal opposition from some of Patrick's neighbours, presumably the ones already enjoying a clear running water supply. A comprehensive sewerage system was required with sewers and covered drains. Pipes were needed to join two springs, supplemented by a reservoir. Middensteads would be removed; every house would have an earth privy (pre-Babbage, up to one in eight) and every three a water closet, (pre-Babbage, none). The many slaughter houses were to be closed and amalgamated into a more hygienically managed one. The toxic graveyard was to be closed under the 1850 Burials Act.

Some of the atrocious housing in Haworth; these are Acton Street and Well Street, demolished in 1970 to become the Changegate car park.

Haworth and its mills

So real Haworth was not quite so romantic a place as many assume it to have been: in 1820 it was an industrial town of 4,600 souls supporting the Yorkshire worsted manufacturers, and in the forty-one years of Patrick's tenure it just continued to grow. The upper storeys of its buildings – built to accommodate weavers and their families – were illuminated by wide windows, necessary so that the men could work at their looms in the upper floor with as much natural light as possible for as long in the day as possible.

The inside of a loom weaver's cottage. Originally published in Costumes of Yorkshire by George Walker.

Turner records (p. 127ff) that Haworth, in 1810, was second only to Bradford (and before Leeds and Halifax) in the amount of wool used in the worsted trade:

> thirty-two persons being numbered among the recipients of drawback, and some of them for high amounts. This was a remission of the tax on soap used in the business. James Greenwood received £90; Joseph Pighills, 64; Sugdenand Heaton, 56; John Feather, 34.

In 1888, 1,200 handlooms were being operated in Haworth, and 600 in Oxenhope, engaged in worsted weaving.

Industrial change and Chartism

We have seen, however, that things were changing and many aspects of textile manufacture were being mechanised and accommodated in the water-powered mills. The balance of the dual economy of agriculture and textile work was shifting and more and more of the local women and children would trudge down the hill to factory jobs in the mills already lining Bridgehouse Beck at the valley bottom. Cottage wool working was rapidly becoming a thing of a past age as the once obligatory spinning wheels and handlooms became redundant. Redundant too were many of the men who were, until now, handloom weavers; while spinning was always women's work, handloom weaving was usually a man's job. Women and children were cheaper labour and it was women and children who the mill owners recruited to fill the jobs in their mills. The depression this caused was deepened by the influx of Irish into the area, fleeing the potato famine; this, combined with local unemployment, only served to fuel Chartism and the associated riots as nearby as Keighley. Physical Force Chartism – its most violent manifestation – was alive and well only eight miles away in Bingley and Bradford. Plug-drawers convened in Haworth and marched through Crossroads, described as 'a riotous mob', but there seems to have been little trouble.

Old Handloom Weavers House, Stanbury.

Chartism was a working-class movement for political reform between 1838 to 1857, borne out of the iniquities inherent in the 1832 Reform Bill. It took its name from the People's Charter of 1838, a petition that called for one vote for every man twenty-one years of age, of sound mind, and not undergoing punishment for a crime; the secret ballot; abolition of property qualifications for MPs to allow the constituencies to return the candidate of their choice; payment of MPs to allow tradesmen, working men, or other persons of modest means to leave or interrupt their livelihood to attend to the interests of the nation; equal electoral districts; and annual elections.

Ebor Mills on fire August 14 2010. © Mark Davis

Ebor Mills in 2010. © Mark Davis

By 1820, there were several major mills in Haworth and Stanbury; they were Ebor and Bridgehouse Mills (1781), which exported to France, on the Bridgehouse Beck (as noted above), New Mill and Hollings Mill on the Sladen Beck, Leeming Mill, built about 1790; Bridge Mill (John and James Greenwood), about 1793 with its 16 horsepower capability; Butterfield and Co.'s Mill, built about 1800, 10horse power; Oxenhope Mill (William Greenwood), built about 1807, 8 horsepower; and Royd House Mill (Jonas Hird), 1819, 8 horsepower. Six further mills were in the River Worth: Ponden, Griffe, Lumb Foot, Springhead, Mytholmes and Vale Mills. Lees Syke and Ivy Bank Mill opened in 1844 and 1860 respectively.

Dunkirk Mill about 1900.

Griffe Mill, Stanbury.

Holme Mill, Laycock.

Oxenhope Mill.

Ivy Bank Lane.

Half of the sixty hands at Bridgehouse in 1833 were under sixteen; some were barely ten. Before the Factories Act hands worked sixty-nine hours per week, twelve hours per day, nine on a Saturday, in a six-day working week; the pay was 5s 11d; there was, unusually, no corporal punishment there, an hour for dinner and eight full days and three half days holiday year, all unpaid; any delays, whatever the cause, had to be made up or wages were docked – conditions at Bridgehouse were enlightened by comparison to many other factories. This was all deemed quite acceptable, a Bingley surgeon even declaring that children had no need of exercise. Greenwood's successor, Richard Butterfield, employed forty-two under sixteen-year-olds and only four adults. Butterfield was a tyrant and a bully whose style of people management caused a strike at his mill; this went to a tribunal of sorts, which found in favour of the workers.

Child workers as published in Costumes of Yorkshire by George Walker.

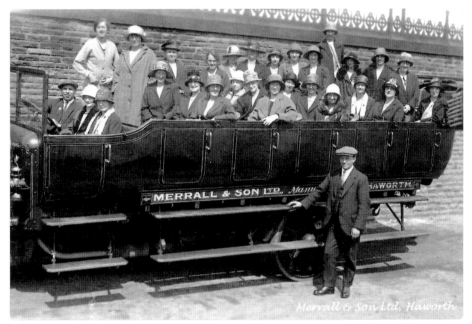

Girls' day out courtesy of Merrall & Sons ...

Although road travel was still very perilous in those days: witness
the Oxenhope Charabanc Disaster on 30 October 1920.

Attempts in 1803 and in the 1820s to improve the lot of the child worker were opposed by the local mill owners.

Depression hit the local trade between the years 1837 and 1842, effectively wiping out the cotton industry. The woollen industry, though, remained essential to Haworth; without the mills there would be no Haworth, but to read the novels and poetry of the Brontës the reader could be forgiven for thinking that industry here was insignificant and impacted little on the village. The reality is that wool sustained Haworth: it was its lifeblood before, during and after the Brontës. In 1820 when the Brontës arrived, it was wool that made Haworth a place that could sustain a number of churches and their congregations. Were there no wool then there would have been no need for Patrick Brontë's services in Haworth.

However, the power loom changed the job market: it made the traditional handloom weaver redundant, their wages progressively reduced to a point where they could not sustain a living. The vast majority of the power loom jobs were taken by women aged between fifteen and twenty-five.

Old Handloom Weavers House near Stanbury.

Croppers and spinners were the first casualties of this Industrial Revolution. They refused to take the loss of their livelihoods lying down and thus precipitated the Luddite riots. Patrick Brontë is believed to have witnessed Luddite activity while curate at Hartshead.

The invention and development of the combing machine dealt another serious blow to the labour market in the 1840s. In 1841 there were 732 combers but the power looms forced many male handloom weavers to convert to wool combing, leaving 302 hand combers by 1861. The resulting reservoir of unemployed men allowed the exploitative mill owners to use them as leverage on their existing, perilously vulnerable labour forces.

Timmy Feather, Stanbury handloom
weaver and legendary clog dancer.

The industrial landscape

In discussing the landscape in Emily Brontë's *Wuthering Heights*, John Bowen is careful to remember that Haworth and its environs were not just wild moors and atrocious weather:

> Yet it is important to remember that Haworth was a modern working town, with several mills and a good deal of industrial unrest. Although it might have seemed distant from London, it was not so far from Manchester (the 'shock city of the age') and the bustling metropolis of Leeds. It was part of a world in rapid motion that witnessed the dramatic mid-Victorian transformation of nature and work in both town and country, changes powered by the railways (for which Branwell Brontë worked) and by the mills that surrounded them.
>
> [John Bowen, *Walking the landscape of Wuthering Heights,* www.bl.uk/romantics-and-victorians/articles/walking-the-landscape-of-wuthering-heights]

The only two of the Brontë sisters' seven novels that deal directly or in any detail with factory workers, with the local textile industry that kept Haworth and its inhabitants alive, are Charlotte's *The Professor* (1846) and her 1849 'Condition of England' novel, *Shirley*. But while that book treats the working poor sympathetically, it is told from the point of view of the comfortably off factory owner and his family.

Branwell, like his Tory-leaning father, had no time for radical thinking in the work place and, consequently, set up an Operative Conservative Party in Haworth in 1837. He fully supported military action against the Chartists who had mustered on the moors above Haworth in 1842 and prayed to God to protect the Conservative government.

This industrial landscape is absent in Anne's novels and in Emily's *Wuthering Heights*. We see it in Charlotte's *Angrian Tales* and in *Ashford*, and she refers to the 1848 bankruptcy of James Greenwood, owner of Bridgehouse Mill, in a letter to Ellen Nussey: 'This is a great and unexpected reverse of fortune — and by throwing many of the poor of Haworth out of employment, has occasioned great distress in the village' [18 August 1848].

But, this and an ambivalent comment in a letter to her father in June 1852 on the strike at Bridgehouse, and what we read in *The Professor* and *Shirley*, is the extent of it. Charlotte is uncompromising in her distaste for Edward Crimsworth's mill in *The Professor*:

> The mill was before us, vomiting soot from its long chimney, and quivering through its thick brick walls with the commotion of its iron bowels [emitting] a dense, permanent vapour.

Robert Moore's 'gaunt mill chimney' in *Shirley* is equally repellent, giving off 'an occasional sulphur-puff from the soot-thick column of smoke'.

Charlotte Brontë knew what she was talking about when it came to green matters, as evidenced by her description to W.S. Williams, literary editor of Smith Elder publishers, of industrial Yorkshire as 'our northern congregations of smoke-dark houses clustered round their soot-vomiting mills'. Blake's 1808 'dark satanic mills' indeed.

Moreover, Charlotte's choice to do her research, not in the mills just down the hill, but over in Birstall and Leeds, could be seen as another instance of her reluctance to associate with the locals.

Deborah Wynne has recently argued:

> that through her early representations of mills and mill owners she formulated an understanding of political conflict and masculine power which helped to shape her mature writing. This culminates in *Shirley* with her critique of the taboo against educated women entering careers in trade and manufacturing.
>
> [Deborah Wynne, *Charlotte Brontë and the Politics of Cloth: The 'Vile Rumbling Mills' of Yorkshire*]

The mill owners in both *The Professor* and *Shirley* bow before Mammon, intent on making profit at the expense of the landscape and the surrounding environment – and, of course at the expense of the workers. To Charlotte, 'there is direct analogy between the moral and physical atmosphere' (*Shirley*), in other words a correlation between industrial pollution and the kind of society that produced it.

The mills in her books and their operation produce not just environmental pollution but moral pollution in the shape of profiteering, materialism, self-interest and greed.

Luddites

Looming in the background to *Shirley* are the violent 1811–1812 Luddite uprisings, which beleaguered the Yorkshire textile industry, causing the destruction of labour-saving machinery and even whole factories. Published under the pseudonym 'Currer Bell', the book is set around Birstall, some six miles south-west of Leeds; in addition to its main theme of industrial unrest, it also examines the role of women in society. So popular was the book that Shirley started to be used as a name for girls; before this, 'Shirley' was usually a boy's name. The Luddites and their successors the Chartists did not draw the line at machinery and factory buildings; they also targeted clergy suspected of sympathising with factory owners; this may be the reason Patrick Brontë always slept with a loaded pistol by his bed. The charge would deteriorate if left neglected, so the vicar of Haworth would fire it out his bedroom window every morning when he got up, and reload each evening.

Luddite insurgency in Newport; 2009 mural of the Newport Rising of 1839. Author: Hughthomas1

The Luddite campaign of violence began in 1812; the workers were incensed by the introduction of new machinery, especially the shear frame, which was making skilled workers, the croppers, redundant. Their concerns matched those of large sections of the poor in general who were restless about the prolonged wars with France and an economic crisis that was putting people out of work and raising food prices. By the summer of 1812, Huddersfield, for example, was virtually an armed camp. By 26 June almost 400 soldiers were stationed there, billeted in public houses; it is suggested that there were at the time more British troops in Yorkshire than Wellington had in Spain. The Luddite campaign of violence included the usual machine smashing and attacks on property; on 28 April 1812, however, the murder of William Horsfall, a local wool textile manufacturer, the owner of Ottiwell's Mill at Marsden and a leading advocate of the new machinery, added a more sinister element to Luddite activism. We can only speculate on what stories Charlotte Brontë may have heard about the mills down the hill from the Parsonage about the troublesome days of 1811 and 1812.

The Leader of the Luddites, 'Ned Ludd'. Published in May 1812 by Messrs Walker and Knight, Sweetings Alley, Royal Exchange; British Museum Working Class Movement Library catalogue.

Rev. John Wade took over from Patrick Brontë in 1861. The 1871 census gives the population as 5,943 showing little increase compared with 1861; but by 1881 it was 6,794 and 7,988 in 1891. 1901 saw little change while 1911 showed a fall to around 7,000. Textile workers accounted for around 68 per cent of the population between 1861 and 1891. The search for work forced a growing disparity in the male/female ratio: in 1861 Haworth had 2,934 males and 2,920 females; thirty years later a gap had widened to 3,766 against 4,222. In 1871, 70per cent of Haworth people were born in Haworth; by 1891 only 54 per cent were. Out-of-work people from the Warwickshire hosiery trade, agricultural depression in Wiltshire and unemployed lead miners from the Yorkshire Dales accounted for much of the influx.

Bill o'th' Hoylus, or William Wright (b. 1836)

This eccentric, picaresque character was born 'in a village midway between Keighley and Haworth', at the Hoylus End houses at Hermit Hole, hence his pen name. Via the National School at Keighley, warp-dressing at a local mill at fourteen, two years in a company of strolling actors and a stint in the West York Rifles where he reached the rank of sergeant, an 1859 marriage and three children, Bill o'th' Hoylus became a pamphleteer writing in a humorous Yorkshire dialect. His oeuvre includes: *History o' Haworth Railway* in 1867, and his *Howorth, Cowenheead, and Bogthorn Almenak*. The cover of this 1873 almanac shows Haworth Church, the Keighley and Worth Valley Railway and the moon; some of the men of Cowling (Cowenheead) reputedly tried to fish the moon out of a dam believing it was made of cheese.

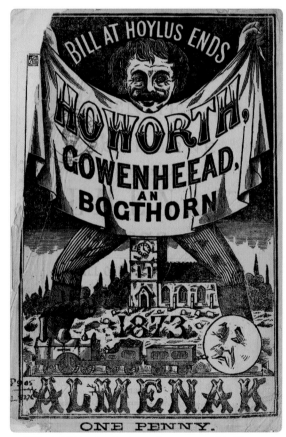

Bill o' th' Hoylus End, on the cover of his Howorth,
Cowenheead, an Bogthorn Almenak for 1873

On 1 February 1853 the roguish Bill o' th' Hoylus End showed off t' War Pig at the Fleece Inn Haworth:

> we'll take this pig to Haworth, and show it as the War Pig from South America … I got 'on tick' a piece of calico several yards long, and with some lampblack I painted in bold type on the calico the words, 'Come and see the War Pig from South America, 2d. each.' … I brought the pig out of the box, and exhibited the animal on a small table in the middle of the room. I introduced the war pig – 'Ladies and gentlemen, – In opening the performance this evening, I have to show you the famous war pig from South America'.
>
> There was an old fellow at the back of the room – a typical old cobbler. He pushed up to the table, and, after 'eyeing' the 'exhibit' somewhat critically through his spectacles, he held forth as follows:- 'Nah, dus ta call thet a war pig?' in the vernacular peculiar to the natives. I said, 'Did ta ivver see a war pig i' thi life?' 'Noa,' said he blankly 'it's t' warst pig I ivver set mi een on.' And then the audience saw where the 'war' pig came in, and they laughed heartily over the joke.

His *Feerful Fire at Howorth* is just as daft:

> In't offices at Bored o' Helth at Howorth a few munths sin thay wor a feerful smell o' gas, so wun on em thowt he see if it let, an went reyt t't meeter we a leeted cannel in his hand, an tuke aht wun at screws, no sooiner had he dun so ner aht brust a leet abaat two yards long; this kaused a gert sensashun; all wor excitement an confushun, t'owd wimmin com runnin aht wi piggins full a watter ta sleck it aht, wun man set off ta Keethla fer t'fire engins, but wen he'd got ta t'Bockin he bethowt him he owt ta hev telegraffed an so he turned back an wen hed gat back he fun thay'd got it aht, by putting a seck ower t'hoil.

THE KEIGHLEY AND WORTH VALLEY RAILWAY

Literary pilgrimages – tourism – became an important source of income, a cash cow for Haworth that was facilitated and boosted by the coming of the Keighley and Worth Valley Railway.

The Keighley and Worth Valley Railway was a five-mile-long branch line that served mills and villages in the Worth Valley; it is now a heritage railway line running from Keighley to Oxenhope connecting to the national rail network at Keighley.

The Flying Scotsman on the Keighley and Worth Valley Railway, 8 April 2017. © Mark Davis

In 1861, John McLandsborough, a civil engineer, visited Haworth to see the place where Charlotte Brontë and her sisters wrote their books. He was astonished (as were probably many other such pilgrims) to find that it was not served by a railway line. McLandsborough proposed a branch running from the Midland station at Keighley to Oxenhope. The line would serve three small towns *en route* and fifteen mills.

A meeting of local gentlemen was convened; the line would cost £36,000 to build, equivalent to £3,080,000 in 2016. The work was scheduled to take about one year, but delays caused by buying land for the line, a cow eating the plans near Oakworth and various engineering problems led to it overrunning by nearly a year. The opening ceremony was held on Saturday 13 April 1867 but, embarrassingly, the train got stuck on Keighley bank and again between Oakworth and Haworth, so that it had to be split before completing its journey. Finally, on 15 April 1867, public passenger services on the Worth Valley line began.

Oakworth

Top of Station Road, Oakworth

Pinewood, Oakworth: Extract from Stanbury School log book:
Last Saturday we had the annual school treat provided by Mrs E H Illingworth of Pinewood, Oakworth. Tea was served to about 80 children at 4:00pm and afterwards we had organised games, children's songs, dances etc. Mrs Edwin recited a parody of the charge of the Light Brigade (Tennyson) & introduced many new games such as Black Magic, guessing games etc. Mr Fred Williams showed how the deaf & dumb speak nowadays with as little hand spelling as possible & recited the Lord's Prayer & a piece of poetry ('That's a Peculiar thing'). Mr Rushworth, a member of the education sub-committee distributed apples & oranges after a short address & then he called for three cheers to Mr & Mrs Illingworth, the donors.

The source of the plan-eating cow? Bill Oth Hoylus End's *History o' Haworth Railway from th' Bcijinnin t' th' End, iri an accant o'th Oppnin Surennini*:

> Oud Blue Beard's nasty wizend kaa
> Hes swellow'd plan o'th railway
> He sed mi blud begins to boil,
> To think et we sud work an toil
> An even th cattle cannot thoyle
> Ta let us hev a railway.
> Began ta think it wur no joak,
> An wisht at greedy kaa ma chouk,
> At swallowd th plan oth railway.

Haworth Steam 2013.
© Mark Davis

British Railways ran the last scheduled passenger train on Saturday 30 December 1961. Freight trains only continued to run to Oxenhope until 18 June 1962. However, all was not lost. A valiant preservation society was formed in 1962 made up of rail enthusiasts and local people, which bought the line from BR and reopened it on 29 June 1968 as the heritage railway we see today. The first train to leave Keighley for Oxenhope on that date was the only train to operate anywhere on the UK network due to a national train strike.

Today, the Keighley and Worth Valley Railway line is a major tourist attraction operated by over 500 volunteers and roughly ten or so paid staff; it carries over 100,000 passengers every year and continues to run steam locomotives along the five-mile branch line from Oxenthorpe, south of Haworth, to the main line at Keighley. In between, it stops at four stations all restored in Edwardian style: at Haworth, Oakworth (where *The Railway Children* was shot), Damens (the smallest working station in Britain) and Ingrow where the Museum of Rail Travel is located.

Haworth station in the 1920s.

The branch line is also home to other organisations:

> Ingrow West Station is also the home of 'Rail Story', a partnership between the Railway, the Vintage Carriages Trust, who have the Museum of Rail Travel here and the Bahamas Locomotive Society whose restoration base and Ingrow Loco Museum are located in the old goods shed. Oxenhope is home to the Lancashire & Yorkshire Railway Trust collection of restored carriages.

The Vintage Carriages Trust (VCT) is particularly focussed on preserving and restoring wooden-bodied carriages.

The Bahamas Locomotive Society (BLS) was formed in 1967 with the aim of purchasing and maintaining in working order the former LMS Railway 'Jubilee' Class 4-6-0 steam locomotive No. 45596 'Bahamas'.

The Lancashire & Yorkshire Railway Trust owns a unique collection of steam locomotives and carriages built by the Lancashire & Yorkshire Railway.

Approaching Oxenhope in 1976.

Oxenhope station.

Near Oxenhope.

CHAPELS AND EDUCATION

By the time of the Brontës' arrival in Haworth, dissident religious worship was well established in the thriving Baptist and Wesleyan chapels, thanks, paradoxically and in no small part, to the fervid evangelical preaching of one of Patrick Brontë's Anglican predecessors, William Grimshaw, incumbent Anglican minister in Haworth parish church from 1742 to 1763. Along with Brontë's Anglican church, the chapels often also provided the village with education and with aspects of its secular social life.

As we have seen, Patrick Brontë preached for forty years from the pulpit of St Michael's Church. In 1851, Patrick's average congregation was about 500 worshippers – very respectable for the times given the population; but the three chapels – Wesleyan and Baptist – drew in three times that between them.

John Wesley (1703–1791) was an Anglican cleric and Christian theologian who, along with his brother Charles Wesley, takes credit for founding the Methodist movement, which began when he started 'field preaching', preaching *al fresco*. John Wesley defiantly challenged the religious assumptions of the day; Methodism was a highly popular evangelical movement that encouraged people to experience Jesus Christ personally.

Before 1800, some Wesleyan Methodists seceded and formed 'a connexion upon Calvinistic principles', a group, that favoured Unitarianism and was later to be known as the Unitarian Baptists. Baptists are a group of denominations and churches that subscribe to a doctrine that baptism should be performed only for professing believers – believer's baptism, as opposed to infant baptism – and that it must be performed by complete immersion and not just affusion or sprinkling.

Charlotte Brontë, as we have seen, complained about the apparent ignorance of the Haworth people. This, though, is hard to reconcile with the strides various church officials, not least her own father, made in advancing educational opportunities in the village. When Patrick Brontë arrived in 1820, he found only one Sunday school, run by the Methodists. The meagre curriculum included only reading, Bible study and a little arithmetic. By 1850 the educational landscape had changed beyond recognition with Sunday school provision by West Lane Baptists (270–480 attendees), Hall Green Baptists (230–300), West Lane Methodists 450–600) and the Anglicans (60–250). The latter two also offered weekday evening classes for children and adults, male and female, and their teachers were professionally trained. The Anglican curriculum included spelling, reading, grammar, ancient and modern history, geography, writing, arithmetic, scriptures and singing – all for 2d a week. The Haworth Free Grammar School taught Greek and Latin, thus opening the all- important doors to Oxford and Cambridge. The Foresters and Mechanics' Institute added to the opportunities on offer with classes, libraries and newspaper reading rooms.

Mill Hey Methodist Chapel

This Primitive Methodists chapel was built in 1836 for Primitive Methodists, a more politically radical branch than the Wesleyan. They began meeting in a cottage in Mill Hill in 1820 and opened the chapel with Sunday school in 1836. The Mill Hey Chapel was closed in 1954.

Haworth West Lane Methodist Church and West Lane Methodist Chapel

Grimshaw's peripatetic and far-reaching preaching brought him into contact with John Wesley and under the influence of Wesley's magnetic style, despite objections from the Vicar of Bradford. Many who later became Methodists had not yet separated from the mainstream church and still worshipped within the Anglican church; but Grimshaw saw that there was a strong desire to break away in many of his congregation.

In 1758, Grimshaw helped to build the West Lane Methodist Chapel to ensure Methodists had a place to worship. The first trustees of the chapel included the Wesley brothers and Grimshaw himself. In Haworth the Methodist tendency was particularly strong and even Patrick Brontë was known to have Methodist leanings and attended West Lane Methodist Chapel with Charlotte to hear the sermons.

At various points in the late eighteenth and early nineteenth century the original West Lane Wesleyan Methodist chapel was rebuilt and enlarged and a Sunday school building added. In the 1950s, declining congregations and increased costs led to the church demolishing the chapel and moving into the adjacent Sunday school building, which is the chapel used today.

It boasts a typically plain interior with a polished wooden alter and pulpit imported from the original chapel. William Grimshaw's chair and an eighteenth-century bronze plaque commemorating the first Methodist chapel are on display.

West Lane Wesleyan (or Methodist) Chapel built in 1853, in about 1895.
The Sunday school is on the left, now the chapel.
On the right is the 1845 chapel demolished in 1951.

West Lane Baptist Chapel

The Worth Valley has a history of dissent that dates back to the seventeenth century. A strong Puritan tradition combined with the independent streak of local yeoman farmers and weavers who were keen to have control of their local church. In 1752 James Hartley formed a Baptist church at West Lane in Haworth. Haworth's first Baptist chapel has its origins in the original West Lane Baptist Church formed in 1752 by a group of people who had broken away from the Established Anglican Church. The original building was declared unsafe, replaced in 1775 and rebuilt again in 1844 with the building that we see today.

Hall Green Baptist Chapel was built in 1824 in the Italian Renaissance style; it retains its galleried interior and original pews. The organ was acquired in 1840. Hall Green Baptist Church was the second Baptist church in the village; why the split no one knows, but by 1821 a number of Baptists were worshipping in a barn at the bottom of the village that still stands to the right of the bridge at the bottom of the hill. Both the West Lane and Hall Green Churches were Strict and Particular Baptist churches, a branch of the church adhering to the doctrine of Calvin.

The Methodists were not just restricted to religious activity: they ran a school in the village from 1821 to which in 1832 the Church of England, under the auspices of Patrick Brontë, reciprocated by building a National School in Church Street as a Sunday school with funds from the National Society and from public subscriptions. Charlotte, Emily, Anne and Branwell all taught there. Charlotte is remembered for upsetting pupils by criticising their needlework. Non-denominational education came to Haworth when the Central Board Schools were built in Butt Lane in 1895.

Haworth was caught up in the prevailing national zeal for self-improvement and horizon-widening. A Philosophical Society was formed in 1780 while orchestral and choral concerts were held in the church and the Black Bull. Highly competitive brass bands were formed by workers in the mills, not least Lumb Foot and Ponden, while musical prowess made good players the target for competing mills. The Haworth Brass Band, formed in 1877, was started at the Springhead Mill in 1854; they still meet in premises next to the Fleece Inn on Main Street.

A snowy Fleece Inn, 27 February 2018. © Mark Davis

A Mechanics' Institute was founded in 1849, providing a library, a newsroom and a lecture hall. Patrick and Charlotte Brontë were both avid supporters of the Institute, which moved in 1853 to new premises, now the Villette Café, in Main Street. Before that The Brontë Society, founded in 1893, opened its first museum in an upper room here in 1895.

The aim of Mechanics' Institutes was to provide a technical education for the working man and for professionals: to 'address societal needs by incorporating fundamental scientific thinking and research into engineering solutions'. They transformed science and technology education for the man in the street. The world's first opened in Edinburgh in 1821 as the School of Arts of Edinburgh, later to become Heriot-Watt University; this was followed in 1823 by the Institute in Glasgow, which was founded on the site of the institution set up in 1800 by George Birkbeck and the Andersonian University offering free lectures on arts, science and technical subjects; it moved to London in 1804, becoming The London Mechanics' Institute from 1823 and, later, Birkbeck College. Liverpool's Institute opened in July 1823 and Manchester (later to become UMIST) in 1824. By 1850, there were over 700 Institutes in the UK and abroad, many of which developed into libraries, colleges and universities.

Mechanics' Institutes were a product of the Industrial Revolution during which, as:

> a consequence of the introduction of machinery a class of workmen emerged to build, maintain and repair the machines on which the blessing of progress depended, at a time when population shifts and the dissolving influences of industrialization in the new urban areas, where

these were concentrated, destroyed the inadequate old apprentice system and threw into relief the connection between material advancement and the necessity of education to take part in its advantages.

[G. Jefferson, *Libraries and Society*, p. 21]

Mechanics' Institutes provided free lending libraries and also offered lectures, laboratories, and occasionally, as with Glasgow, a museum.

School Diaries and Log Books provide invaluable information about the day-to-day activities in schools, but at the same time adumbrate aspects of contemporary educational practice and local social history. Here are some random examples from three of Haworth's schools:

Haworth Wes. Infant School Diary/ Log Book 1864 – 1895

Here we learn of such miscellaneous issues as special needs provision, or 'dull scholars who are to receive special attention'; 'dull' marching lessons; the, by our cultural norms, casual attitude towards death; persistently smelly pupils, and swearing in class.

1864

Tuesday	Apr 12th	Admitted 2 new ones.
Wednesday	Apr 13th	In the afternoon we had a walk on the moors.
Thursday	Apr 14th	Cautioned a monitor against fighting.
Wednesday	Apr 27th	The children have been restless. I attribute it to the weather.
Monday	June 13th	A moral lesson. Subject: Stealing.
Tuesday	June 21st	The writing is better.
Wednesday	June 29th	Numbers low on account of wet weather.
Monday	Oct 31st	Punished a boy for spending his school money. Moral lesson.

1867

Friday	Feb 1st	Gave a special marching lesson.
Wednesday	Feb 20th	Formed a class of dull scholars who are to receive special attention.
Thursday	Feb 28th	Gave a lesson on the 'Monkey'. Children much interested and pleased.
Monday	Mar 15th	Many children have the measles & the weather is rough so our numbers are low at present.
Friday	Mar 26th	Gave special attention to a few backward children.
Wed	Oct 2nd	Had no playtime today it being very wild weather.
Fri	Oct 3rd	Learned the words 'God save the Queen' with the tune.
Nov 5th		Closed at 3 o' clock it being the fifth of November.
Nov 21st		Had a marching lesson instead of playtime because of the cold.

Dec 9th	Children could not walk to school today, the ground being all slippery with the strong frost so that we have had scarcely any scholars to begin with for the week.
Dec 19th	Finish today for Christmas holidays. One of the scholars died this week.

1892

Mar 25th	One boy who is eight years old, has been absent from school twelve months with a broken leg & is therefore very backward.

1893

Jan 6th	F. Pickles gave a 'fair' lesson on a railway station.
July 7th	We gave a holiday yesterday because of the Royal Wedding.
Aug 25th	We have lost several families, owing to the bad trade.
Nov 3rd	There is a decrease in attendance this week, owing to the prevalence of Chicken-Pox

1894

Jan 19th	Whooping cough & chicken pox are very bad in the district.
June 22nd	The routine was interrupted on Wednesday morning, when the children were photographed.
June 29th	We closed school at 3 o'clock on Wednesday afternoon & took all the children on the Moor, where they had games & a scramble of nuts, sweets etc.
Sept 14th	Admitted two girls & one boy this morning; the children of worthless parents.

1899

Jan 6th	Have sent a boy – H. Mitchell – home, with a note, on account of his being dirty and smelling of something, which scented the whole room. Miss Lund, his teacher, has complained repeatedly of him.
Jan 10th	The boy Mitchell, being no better, has been sent home again.
Jan 19th	I had to severely reprimand a boy for swearing while at play.
Dec 11th	The committee have provided a piano for the use of the Infants room, I find it improves the order, & makes the dull & marching very much more interesting.

1897

Feb 19th	Miss Simpson gave a lesson on 'The Dragon Fly'
Nov 21st	… I have had specially to speak to Miss Blakey, about her mechanical style of questioning & teaching generally.

This afternoon I had to punish R. Hudson severely. I had warned the school several times against snow-balling in the yard at play-time. This boy ignored my warning this afternoon, and denying he had done so, I punished him smartly.

Central Board Schools, Haworth

The school was built in 1896 and opened on 1 March 1897. Here, we learn of teachers turning up late, a family bereavement with little time off in consequence, a serious breach of staff discipline, serious supply shortages, that all-important new door mat, and a case of kleptomania.

1890

Jan 21st	On account of the alarming reports of her Majesty, opened school by singing the National Anthem.
Jan 24th	A lesson on the life of Queen Victoria has been given in all the classes to-day. After the lesson each child wrote or copied a letter to their parents, containing an account of the lesson.
Jan 30th	Left school this morning, having received a telegram from the Bingley & Keighley joint Hospital, that my eldest daughter was dangerously ill.
Feb 1st	Away on account of death of my daughter.
Feb 4th	Many children away sick.
Mar 27th	Lessons on 'The Census' given to remaining classes.
Apr 19th	Have not taken cookery this week, owing to the age limit in New Code.
May 15th	M. Kershaw, sent home this morning, could not see to make out a fraction sum, from print, as she had not brought her 'glasses'.
July 17th	On the advice of Medical Officer of Health, the school is closed until end of the summer holidays, owing to prevalence of whooping cough.
Oct 18th	Enoch Chaplin, not having been once absent in 4½ years, was presented by the teachers and scholars of his class with a book.

1900

Mar 13th	Miss Hudson was guilty of a serious breach of discipline this morning. As a consequence of which she went home.

1905

Feb 20th	Part timers are playing at the mill in turns. Am insisting upon their attendance at school when not at the mill.
Apr 7th	Reading in the lower division is very weak. Few can phrase, and the vowel effects in single syllables not at all well known.
May 10th	We are suffering inconvenience from delay of apparatus. We are now without ink & pens.
Aug 28th	Mr Long, having missed his train, did not get to school until 9.25. This was also the case last Monday morning.
Aug 30th	Lessons on 'solar eclipse' given to all classes. Took scholars into yard at 11.45 – each with perforated paper. Unfortunately, the sky was overcast.

Sep 7th	Haworth visited by a party of Frenchmen from Surcene? Gave the whole school a short address on 'L'entente Cordiale'.
Oct 23rd	Special lesson to all classes on 'Nelson & Trafalgar'.
Oct 31st	Lesson on 'The Gunpowder Plot' throughout the school: also a 'composition' on the subject.

Haworth Central Board School, 1915.

1922

Aug 28th	Re-opened. All staff presence, except Mr J. Barrett, who has happened a severe motor accident during the holiday. He will, probably, be away between two & three months.
Sep 8th	During this week I have been much exercised with a boy in St.1 (William Waddington) who seems afflicted with Kleptomania. Have discussed the case with the staff.
Sep 20th	We have had repeated trouble with the little boy William Waddington. He has been examined by our Dr Wakon, and reported to medical department at County Hall.

1926

| November 2nd | All but the few children who were wearing Wellington boots had wet feet. Teachers were occupied until 10.30 a.m. with drying shoes and stockings. |

At noon a girl was bit on the arm, by a dog which had followed two boys into the cloakroom. The bite caused a bad bruise. It was treated with peroxide & iodine. The nurse afterwards examined it, it is not likely that any ill effects will follow.

Nov 11th	At morning assembly H.T. gave a little talk on the meaning of Armistice Day. At 10.55 a.m. the school again assembled in the hall, and at 11 o'clock for two minutes silence was observed.
Nov 23rd	Interview Dr Lindsay, school doctor re a mentally defective child who had been presented for admission upon his advice. After keeping the child under observation for an hour and half the doctor asked the parent to keep her at home for 12 months.

1927

Feb 21st	Dr Lindsay visited for routine inspection, attendance 99. Of those examined, he excluded immediately, 5 whom he found had high temperatures and one girl who had Chicken Pox. He telephoned to Dr Atkinson re closure of school owing to prevalence of influenza. The clerk to the U.D.C. sent a messenger ordering closure for this week. Scholars were dismissed at once and attendance cancelled for the morning.
June 17th	An American lady, formerly a teacher, visited this afternoon, she wished to compare American & English methods.
Aug 29th	A scholar aged five (? Clarke) has died during the weekend.
Aug 30th	40 large bunches of beautiful flowers were brought by scholars to send to the funeral of their deceased playing mate.
Sep 26th	Mr Bailey reports several cases of illness – one whooping cough and two of swollen glands.

1928

Mar 22nd	While trying to open a window with a map pole this afternoon the Head Teacher cracked and slightly broke a pane of glass in one of the windows in Room 5.
Apr 24th	This morning a new door mat has arrived.

Junior Mixed & Infants' C. School, Haworth

There were much the same issues here but activities were obviously affected and influenced by the war; there was one case of indecent exposure, the first day of school dinners, Schick testing and a whistleblower reporting a fellow teacher stealing the milk.

1941

Feb 7th	H.T. carried out inspection of Gas Masks.
Feb 10th	Air Raid practices renewed after long spell of bad weather.
May 20th	Mr Dove H.M.I. visited. New air raid shelters were the cause of his visit.
June 9th	Influx of evacuees from Hull & London.
Aug 25th	During the holidays the death occurred, of Susannah Harrison who was in charge of Class 6 (junior) up to the last day of term.

1942

Apr 17th   All Gas Masks in school tested. Seventeen children needed small Civilian Respirators in place of Mickey Mouse type. Twenty three children had respirators which were damaged and they were instructed to obtain replacements.

Jun 17th   H.T. of Senior school visited p.m. with reference to a case of indecent exposure by an elderly man witnessed by children in this school in company with senior school children. Two children were interviewed and gave information concerning the occurrence.

Sep 30th   From school funds a Radio Pick Up for the gramophone was purchased this day and fixed to gramophone. This amplifies sound and makes it possible to use records for certain lessons more easily.

Oct 14th   A Cinema Projector (Ensign 300B 16 mm Silent) has been purchased from school funds – jointly with youth group.

Nov 9th   Films were shown to upper-class a.m. and lower classes p.m.

The films shown were (1) Fish from the sea; (2) Heavy industries; (3) Jamaican harvest; (4) The life of the tawny Owl.

Nov 13th   Films from the education office arrived unexpectedly this morning. The films shown on this occasion were (a) The tide; (b) Cocoa from the Golden Coast; (b) The romance of the Swan.

1943

Feb 1st   Provision of school dinners commenced this day. First menu consisted of Roast Beef, Boiled and Baked Potatoes, Peas. Ginger Pudding and Custard.

Feb 8th   Mrs Florence Shuttleworth (née Rushworth) Reg No. 21/2678 commenced duties as 'Supply' this a.m.

Apr 1st   D.E & F., gave 'Schick' test to six children. [The Schick test is a test using an intradermal injection of diphtheria toxin to determine whether or not a person is susceptible to diphtheria. It was named after its inventor, Béla Schick (1877–1967), a Hungarian-born American paediatrician.]

June 21st   It is also learned today that Miss Enid Roper has been appointed 3rd horn player in the Halle Orchestra and will, in all probability be leaving us at the end of the week.

1944

Jan 25th   Mrs Matthews reported finding of milk bottle containing ⅓ pint of milk in a teacher's bag. Head teacher reluctantly took up investigation without really satisfactory result.

Jan 26th   In afternoon, Mrs Matthews, teacher in charge in Nursery sent for head teacher and again reported taking of milk by a teacher.

	This time unfortunately the case was only too clear teacher being actually on way home with a bottle of milk. After reprimanding teacher for repeating an offence which she formally denied head teacher sent brief report to the Director.
Jan 31st	Director of Education called a.m. re- teacher and the matter of stolen milk. The director stated that he had interviewed the teacher at the office on Saturday last and following a very abject apology had promised her that the matter would be forgotten if she would promise to see that the incident was not repeated. That promise had been given.
June 6th	Invasion of Europe by allied forces began this morning.
June 12th	Pudding delivered for school dinners today in rusted tins. Jam on pudding had turned black. Attention drawn to this by head teacher who took sample of a pudding and specimen lid to Education Office.

During afternoon Miss C. Bancroft had trouble with child who swore at her. Head teacher called in to deal with child who has been a constant source of trouble recently. Head teacher slapped child (on seat) and put him in office. Child's mother, who happened to be about school during play time came to head teacher's office and caused scene, waxing most abusive at times. Mr R.M. Bailey, who was also present was witness to her abusive manners. Finally calmed by head teacher and having heard boy's own confession as to his class behaviour, agreed that child had been troublesome and would have taken him home to punish him. However, head teacher refused this and took child to Miss Bancroft to apologise.

Sep 13th	Dr Marshall visited nursery a.m. and found a girl to have slight attack of Scabies. As a result she saw her sister in junior department, whom she found to have bad attack. Both excluded.

1945

24th January	Head teacher complained to Food Van Drivers about kind of food delivered and ordered them to take it back to centre. Van driver refused, insolently. Helper used bad language. Head teacher reported both food and van drivers to Education Office.
22nd February	This afternoon 2.45 to 4.0 p.m. Mr H. Mitchell, curator of the Brontë Museum came into school to give a lecture (illustrated by his own episcope pictures) on the Brontës and Haworth. The children were most attentive and greatly enjoyed the lecture (given to the top class Junior IV only.)
7th May	In view of the report, by radio, of the surrender of Germany and the imminence of V.E (Victory in Europe) Day, the head teacher called all classes together and announced that in all probability school would be closed tomorrow and the next day. Prayers were offered for our deliverance and our victory and the school dismissed at 4:05pm.

11th September In connection with V.J. celebrations tea was supplied to all children in school by V.J. Committee and served by members of W.V.S. and school staff. In the evening an entertainment in the form of a Punch and Judy show with ventriloquist and conjuring acts was provided after sports for school children.

1947

10th September Reported dangerous condition of staff lavatory.

24th October School closed p.m. for autumn holiday of one week. Head teacher issued usual warning re- safety-first and found on inquiry that more than 60% of children would be left alone in house during the holiday.

3rd November Many children absent due to an epidemic of mumps.

8th July, 1949 Punished boys for slinging water at each other. As boys grinned and giggled about punishment I ordered them to stand before my desk while I continued with work. ___ began to make others laugh so gave him second stroke on seat. A few minutes later he appeared ill and vomited. I gave him water to drink and he recovered.

6th March, 1950 Admitted this day a Dutch boy and a Lithuanian girl. Neither child able to speak more than two or three words of English.

OTHER HAWORTH BUILDINGS AND INSTITUTIONS

The Freemasons have had a presence in Haworth since the end of eighteenth century when the Prince George Lodge first convened at the Old White Lion at the top of the village. The members moved to the Three Graces when, in 1812, the Prince George moved away to the Calder Valley. The Three Graces Lodge No. 48 initially met at the nearby Black Bull; by 1812 the two lodges had amalgamated, later moving to the King's Arms in 1821, the White Lion and then to private rooms in Newell Hill in 1833, now Lodge Street. Branwell Brontë was proposed and accepted into the Masonic lodge here on 29 February 1836, becoming secretary in 1837. His last recorded meeting was in 1842. In 1907 the lodge moved to Mill Hey. The Lodge at Mill Hey was built in 1907 and held its first meeting in December of that year. It survives as a Masonic lodge to this day.

There was also a Good Templars' Lodge and a Conservative Club. In the days before sickness benefit and life assurance and the like, benefits clubs were set up to pay sickness and funeral benefits and widows' pensions. The earliest in Haworth was the 1781 New Union Society.

The Ancient Order of Foresters were established in 1846, meeting in their own rooms, the Sun and in the Black Bull.

The Victoria Hall was built in 1854 next to the Hall Green Baptist Chapel and, along with the New Inn, was a meeting place for the Oddfellows Friendly Society. **The Woodlands Lodge of the Ancient Order of Oddfellows** was and is a politically and religiously independent society. There is nothing odd about the name. Odd Fellows (or Oddfellows, Odd Fellowship or Oddfellowship), is an international fraternity consisting of lodges first documented in 1730 in London, the first known lodge being Loyal Aristarcus Lodge No. 9. Convivial meetings were held 'in much revelry and, often as not, the calling of the Watch to restore order'. The names of several pubs today would indicate past Odd Fellows affiliations. The name 'odd fellows' may come from people who practised 'odd trades', who joined together to form a larger group of 'odd fellows'. Even today, Odd Fellows espouse philanthropy, reciprocity, mutual assistance and charity.

Our Lady of Lourdes is the first Catholic church in Haworth, built in 1925. Before then, Catholics would have to travel to Keighley to attend mass. During the First World War when fuel was rationed the priest came to his flock and mass was regularly conducted in an upstairs room of a draper's shop on Mill Hey, belonging to the Pedley family.

The Parish is twinned with the Parish of St Joseph, Matli in Pakistan, and supports a TB outreach programme there.

Minnie Street was home to the **Drill Hall** built in 1873 to provide training facilities for the Haworth Company of the 42nd Company of the West Yorkshire Rifle Volunteers. An invasion scare in 1859 led to the creation of the Volunteer Force; there was considerable local enthusiasm for joining the local Rifle Volunteer Corps (RVCs) in 1866.

The Sun Inn in West Lane was where turnpike road tolls were collected in the mid-nineteenth century.

The Fold, West Lane, was a good example of the chronic overcrowding in Haworth: in 1851 there were eight households here with fifty-two inhabitants crammed in; nine of them were lodgers in a lodging house run by a handloom weaver.

The 'square' at the top of Main Street is where the old village stocks were. No. 121 was the post office during the time of the Brontës; No. 123 was a temperance hotel, keenly supported by Patrick Brontë who was President of Haworth's Temperance Society. Opposite is Rose's Apothecary, an impressive building with smooth ashlar masonry. The Black Bull and the Old White Lion, rebuilt in 1858, were also here.

The Old Apothecary (Rose's) is where Branwell Brontë bought his laudanum; it was a druggist shop then, run by Betty Hardacre. Laudanum is a tincture of opium containing approximately 10 per cent powdered opium by weight (the equivalent of 1 per cent morphine). It contains almost all of the opium alkaloids, including morphine and codeine, making it a powerful narcotic painkiller, sold then legally without prescription.

© Mark Davis

Today, the Old Apothecary is an attractive Victorian-style store including authentic polished mahogany display cases, glass bottles, antique advertisements and gas lighting.

As for **the Parsonage**, Patrick's successor, Rev. Wade, added the gabled wing in 1878.

Through the archway next to Emma's Café was **Gauger's Croft**. In the Brontës' day, this was another suffocatingly packed area of terraced housing, with a number of cellar dwellings. These houses were demolished as part of a slum clearance campaign in the 1960s.

'Villette' in Main Street was built in 1853, originally as a lecture room for the Black Bull, then the Mechanics' Institute and after that the Liberal Club. The most impressive shop fronts in Main Street are probably at Nos 75 and 77, built in 1854.

Central Park between Burr and Bridgehouse Lane opened in 1929; brass band concerts were performed in a bandstand there.

Park and bandstand.

Haworth Old Hall

This early seventeenth-century house is now a pub and restaurant with real fires blazing out of two magnificent original fireplaces. Formally known as Emmott Old Hall, the building has changed hands many times between local landowning families.

There are vaulted cellars underneath the building that were once connected to tunnels used as escape routes for priests, and later by other non-conformists who used the building as a meeting house. The Emmott family were recusants, but they did not inherit the Old Hall until 1746.

In its time the Old Hall has seen service as a court house, private dwelling and now a public house and restaurant. Much of the building retains original features: a heavy oak door opens into the bar area with stone flag floors and polished oak beams. The dining room is in what was the grand hall of the house.

Old Haworth Old Hall.

And in 2010. © Mark Davis

Below the hall was a green, known as Hall Green, on which was the ancient **Ducking Stool** Pond where punishment was exacted on scolds, brawling women and dishonest bakers.

Woodlands, Sun Street: built by the Greenwood family, of Bridgehouse Mills, in 1832. A private drive gives access to the house and after 1867 a bridge was built over the railway and the Bridgehouse Beck to provide direct access to the factory.

Ivy Bank Mills: this mill, now derelict, was built for worsted spinning in about 1870.

Bridgehouse Mills was originally water-powered and used for worsted yarn spinning; steam power and weaving sheds later additions. Only the frontage buildings survive dating from the mid and late nineteenth century.

Bridgehouse Mills in later days.

The War Memorial, Bridgehouse: 105 men from Haworth village lost their lives in the First World War.

Mill Hey and Brow: Mill Hey was originally a group of cottages near to the corn mill on the Bridgehouse Beck. When the railway came Brow developed in 1867 to form a settlement distinct from Haworth village. The settlement had its own chapels, Sunday schools, shops, a police station and, by the early twentieth century, two cinemas: the 1913 Hippodrome, on Belle Isle (now flats) and the Brontë, which opened in 1921.

William Smith with goose and cautious child in May Street, Brow.

Howarth Brow and the gasworks.

Mill Hey.

Mill Hey showing the Royal Oak.

ST MICHAEL AND ALL ANGELS' CHURCH

The Corpse Path leading past the Sunday school to the church. © Mark Davis

The church we see today is the third church building on the site, built between 1879 and 1881, although parts, notably the tower, survive from the original medieval building. The church is best known, of course, for its connection with Rev. Patrick Brontë who was minister of the parish between 1820 and 1861.

We have records of a chapel on the site from 1488, although there is an earlier reference, at the Archbishop's office in York, to a command that in 1137 the rector of Bradford and the people of Haworth pay the curate officiating in the chapel. A later church was built in 1488; traces of this building remain in the lower part of the church tower.

The church in snow on 27 February 2018. © Mark Davis

William Grimshaw was appointed parson in 1742; he was something of a pioneer of the evangelical style of preaching and brought a breath of fresh air to sermonising; Turner (p. 52) tells us that

> Mr. Grimshaw may be considered one of the most hard-working and conscientious clergymen of his age, in the north of England. The labours he accomplished in the way of preaching, and other religious exercises, in Howarth and neighbouring parishes, are extraordinary. He was one of the most enthusiastic disciples of John Wesley, who often preached in Haworth Church and the churchyard to overflowing congregations. Though Mr. Grimshaw, on many occasions, exhibited more zeal than judgment, yet he was much respected by all parties in Haworth, and succeeded, though often by the persuasion of a horse-whip, in putting down there many rank vices. His popularity so increased the congregation that it was necessary to enlarge the church, which was accomplished in 1755.

Grimshaw's cottage, Sowdens.

In his diary for 1748 Wesley notes that:

> At eight I preached at Eccleshill, and about one at Keighley. At five Mr. Grimshaw read prayers and I preached at Haworth, to more than the Church could contain. We began the service in the morning (Thursday, 25th) at five, and even then the Church was nearly filled ... Wednesday, June 30th, 1753,I rode to Haworth, where Mr. Grimshaw read prayers, and I preached to a crowded congregation; but, having preached ten or twelve times in three days, besides meeting the societies, my voice began to fail.

Grimshaw soon realised the problems of gathering a flock in Haworth made up of farmers and handloom weavers, largely scattered across the hills and valleys in small hamlets and isolated farmhouses. So Grimshaw got on his horse and rode the length and breadth of his parish preaching peripatetic passionate outdoor sermons. They struck a chord with his largely illiterate parishioners who relished the rousing hymn singing and fervent prayers. Grimshaw was soon conducting thirty to forty services a week as far afield as Pateley Bridge in the east and Colne to the west.

Turner (p. 54) cannot underestimate the massive spiritual contribution he believes Grimshaw made to the spiritual development of the people of Haworth; to Turner, Grimshaw *was* Haworth:

> The name of Haworth, would scarcely be known at a distance, were it not connected with the name of Grimshaw. The bleak and barren face of the adjacent country was no improper emblem of the state of the inhabitants; who in general had little more sense of religion than their cattle, and were wild and uncultivated like the rocks and mountains which surrounded them. By the blessing of God upon Mr. Grimshaw's ministry, this desert soon became a fruitful field, a garden of the Lord, producing many trees of righteousness, planted by the Lord himself, and the barren wilderness rejoiced and blossomed like the rose.

Had Turner forgotten about the Brontë sisters, or does it indicate perhaps how blasé and disinterested the locals were of the Brontë phenomenon on their doorstep?

It is easy to see how the Grimshaw effect was a powerful influence on the fast-emerging non-conformist religions, not least the early Methodists for whom he organised meetings into a circuit known as the Great Haworth Round. Many of his converts eventually became Methodists or Baptists and established new chapels and Sunday schools across the region.

Back at St Michael's, Grimshaw became a victim of his own success: his parish church could not accommodate the booming congregation; accordingly, he applied his religious zeal to energetic fundraising and by 1756 had raised sufficient funds to extend the church. Typical high-sided box pews, an imposing organ and a three-tiered pulpit were all installed along with first floor galleries with extra seating.

This was what Patrick Brontë found on the church when he arrived in 1820. Tragically, and ironically, Grimshaw's son, like Brontë's, was addicted to drink until shortly before his death. After acquiring his father's horse, he used to say 'it once carried a saint, now it carries a devil'.

Inside the church. © Mark Davis   Outside the church. © Mark Davis

Patrick Brontë arrived in Haworth with his wife, Maria, and the children in 1820 from their home in Market Street, Thornton, having been offered the perpetual curacy of the church by the vicar of Bradford the year before. In his forty-one years in post he was assisted at Haworth from 1845 by his son-in-law, Arthur Bell Nicholls (1819–1906) as curate. Nicholls later married Charlotte Brontë.

Brontë was succeeded by Rev. Wade who in 1879 had all but the clock tower of the old church demolished and rebuilt as it is today. The 1879 rebuild caused a degree of righteous indignation amongst many parishioners, presumably those who had commercial interests in the village, fearful of the effect it would have on the celebrity then enjoyed by the parsonage and the Brontë sisters. Others in the village, though, supported the scheme, concerned that their church had become impossibly cluttered and worried about the infectious and toxic drainage from the churchyard silently percolating underneath the church.

Inside St Michael's there is a stained glass window dedicated 'To the Glory of God in pleasant memory of Charlotte Brontë by an American citizen' and a plaque on a pillar indicating the location of the Brontë family vault. Today, visitors from all over the world continue to flock to the church to see the Brontë Memorial Chapel and the Brontë family tomb where all the Brontë family with the exception of Anne are buried. The tomb is marked by a simple plaque from 1882. The chapel was built in 1963.

The plaque. © Mark Davis   © Mark Davis

In 1864, A.J. Putnam received a guided tour from the then sexton, in effect pointing out what visitors still see today:

> In the morning, after breakfast, I went to the church in company with the warden and sexton. They showed me the church-records in which Mr. Nicholls and Charlotte wrote their names when they were married. The high pulpit in which old Mr. Brontë continued to preach after he had become blind, and to which he was generally led from the house by Charlotte, stands against one of the side-walls; and in front of it are lower desks for the clerk and precentor. There are galleries at the right of the speaker, and in front on the other side. Beneath the gallery, at the right, is the mural tablet of the Brontë Family, on which are inscribed all their names: close by, beneath the stones of the aisle, repose their bodies. Opposite the tablet, and just across the aisle, is the family pew, —plain, square, and high. They pointed out the seat in one corner where Charlotte invariably sat, a constant attendant and a devout worshipper. Here, in this pew, the old father and the afflicted husband stood and saw all that was mortal of the pride and the glory of their house lowered into the grave. 'Ah!' said the good old sexton to me, 'it was a very melancholy spectacle'.

> [A.J. Putnam (1864) 'A Visit at Haworth',
> *The Monthly Religious Magazine* 31, 41–46]

THE GRAVEYARD

A dreary, dreary place literally paved with rain-blackened tombstones.

[Bessie Parkes, a visitor around 1850]

Ellen Nussey felt the same bleak gloom:

> The Passing-Bell was often a dreary accompaniment to the day's engagements … you looked upon the Stone-cutter's chipping shed which was piled with slabs ready for use, and to the earth there was the incessant sound of the chip, chip of the recording chisel as it graved in the Memoriams of the departed.

[*Reminiscences*, 1871]

The graveyard was a tourist attraction in its own right at the end of the nineteenth century.

The graveyard, church school buildings, sexton's house and the Parsonage are next to the church. The graveyard is believed to accommodate between 40,000 and

42,000 bodies in an area of less than one acre; in 1850, Babbage in his report calculated that 1,344 people had been buried there since 1840. From 1605 it was the tradition to remove the older bones and deposit them on the annual autumn bone-fire. Because of the overcrowding the graveyard was closed in 1856 with a new cemetery opening just off the Stanbury road. Patrick Brontë campaigned for the original graveyard to be cleaned up and have the headstones placed vertically to improve the poor drainage and expedite decomposition. Ranks of sloping or flat gravestones were restored to the vertical to allow shrubs to grow and improve decomposition of the bodies; trees were planted around and within the site in 1865 to further improve drainage. Indeed, Sundays excepted, the care of the deceased easily outweighed the care of the living with an endless stream of funeral services, grave-digging, headstone engraving, coffin ordering, bell tolling and so on.

In 1865, J. Tomlinson recorded his bitter personal experience of the burial ground:

> The church-yard stands above the houses, and the Moors above the church-yard; so that water from the rocky moor-land springs, percolates through the graves into the village, and the inhabitants drink it. Drat it! My mouth might well be feverish, for had I not used water with the rum?
>
> [J. Tomlinson (1865) 'Haworth, where the Brontës Lived', *Some interesting Yorkshire Scenes*, London, 116–154]

Four atmospheric photos of the graveyard; February 27 2018. © Mark Davis

Indeed, the graveyard in some ways has a life of its own. It was, as we noted, a conduit for the foul, toxic water that surreptitiously bled into the local water supply. It was also home to a number of graves with some astonishing facts within them. Having bewailed the frighteningly short life expectancy in Haworth we come across the remarkable longevity enjoyed by the Murgatroyd family: Susan, wife of John, 1785, aged 86; John, 1789, aged 88; James, their son, 1820, aged 95, Ann, his wife, 1831, aged 85; Sarah, wife of John, 1846, aged 70, and John (son of James), 1862, aged 85. Combined ages 509. The Beavers too, of Butteryate Sike, enjoyed long lives: Thomas died 1727, aged 76; Paul, his son, 1767, aged 83; Jonas his ion 1788, aged 82; Paul, brother of Jonas, 1786, aged 77.

A headstone near the back window of the Black Bull Inn has the inscription: J.S. 1796. J.S. was hanged for stealing. Nearby, there is a stone to the memory of five women who were not worth the expense of the mason etching their names …

> Here lie the Bodies of the 5 Wives of William Sunderland. Also William Sunderland 1790.

… while the five-times widower gets two mentions. The oldest stone in the graveyard dates back to 1642 to commemorate I.H.

But it is the families that suffered multiple bereavements that are the most disturbing: Grave D/435 entombs the remains of Richard and Mary Whitaker – and their sixteen children, from Frances aged nineteen to Michael aged two; twelve siblings are unnamed. We also know that Patrick Brontë performed the funeral ceremony for Sarah Burwin and seven of her children – the eldest twenty-eight, the youngest seven. In E/515 lie the seventeen children of Joseph and Mary Leeming: those aged six, four and two are named; the rest remain nameless. At D/028 the father of the seven Heaton children was moved to create a poignant sculpture of a child asleep in a bower in memory of his infants.

© Mark Davis

THE REVEREND PATRICK BRONTË

'An able and faithful clergyman'

Patrick Brontë (born Brunty, 1777–1861), Irish priest and author, is most famous for being the father of the Brontë sisters and Branwell, their brother. Before theology and the church he took on several apprenticeships consistent with his humble background – to a blacksmith, a linen draper, and a weaver – before becoming a teacher in 1798 when he opened a school; this he kept going for five years when he became tutor in the family of the Rev. Mr Tighe, at Drumgooland in 1802. Moving to England in 1802, he read divinity and ancient and modern history at St John's College, Cambridge, graduating with a BA in 1806 – an achievement all the more remarkable given that his father, Hugh Brunty, was an agricultural labourer with the limited financial means that went with such an occupation. While at Cambridge, he joined a company of volunteers intended to repel the threatened invasion by Napoleon; among his comrades were Lord Palmerston and the late Duke of Devonshire. The last time the Duke visited his seat at Bolton Abbey, he called on Mr Brontë, at Haworth, and a few days afterwards sent some hampers of game and other delicacies.

Brontë's first appointment was as curate at Wethersfield, near Braintree in Essex, where he was ordained a deacon of the Church of England in 1806, and into the priesthood in the following year. In 1809, he moved to Wellington, Shropshire, where he was assistant curate, and in 1810 his first published poem, 'Winter Evening Thoughts', was published in a local newspaper, followed in 1811 by a collection of moral verses, *Cottage Poems*. He moved to the West Riding of Yorkshire in 1811 as assistant curate at Hartshead, until 1815. In the meantime (1812) he was appointed a school examiner at a Wesleyan academy, Woodhouse Grove School, near Guiseley. On 25 February 1820 he moved on to become perpetual curate of Thornton.

Longstanding servants confirmed that Mr Brontë 'was one of the kindest men that ever drew breath'. It seems that here was nothing too good for his family and servants. These were the two servants later stigmatised by Mrs Gaskell as 'wasteful', but were amply vindicated by Mr Brontë in 1857, when he said, 'Mrs Gaskell has made us appear as bad as she could'.

It was at Guiseley that the reverend met Maria Branwell (1783–1821), whom he married on 29 December 1812. Miss Branwell 'was exceedingly small in person, not pretty, but very elegant, and always dressed with a quiet, simplicity of taste'.

She possessed considerable literary taste and brought her husband an annuity of £50 a year.

Their first child, Maria and their second, Elizabeth (1815–1825), died in childhood after the family had moved to Thornton. Both Maria and Elizabeth had attended the austere and unforgiving Clergy Daughters' School at Cowan Bridge near Kirkby Lonsdale; both suffered hunger, cold, and neglect there. In the wake of an outbreak of typhoid, Maria came home with tuberculosis, and died aged eleven on 6 May 1825. Elizabeth died on 15 June 1825 within two weeks of coming home.

According to Turner (pp. 84–85), a servant has said that Maria was:

> a grave, thoughtful and quiet girl. She was delicate and small in appearance, which seemed to give greater effect to her wonderful precocity of intellect. She must have been her mother's companion and helpmate … between seven and eight Maria would read the newspaper, and be able to report 'debates in Parliament'. She was as good as a mother to her sisters and brother.

Turner (p. 85) tells us that Brontë was a solitary man, bordering on the misanthropic; however, he obviously had his children's best interests at heart because:

> Mr. Brontë taught his children their lessons when young. Besides his attention to their minds, he wished to make them hardy, and indifferent to the pleasures of eating and dress.

He was one of those men who, in some respects, would never win, no matter what he did:

> He fearlessly took whatever side in local or national politics appeared to him right. On account of his opposition to the Luddites, he became unpopular (for a time) among the millworkers about Hartshead, and then, as was necessary, began to carry a loaded pistol about with him, a practice he continued through life … Afterwards he offended the mill-owners because he took the part of the workpeople in a 'strike'.

The four remaining children were born in Thornton: Charlotte (1816–1855), Patrick Branwell (1817–1848), Emily (1818–1848) and Anne (1820–1849).

Charlotte's register of birth.
© Mark Davis

Charlotte and Emily, too, had to endure the hell that was Cowan Bridge, suffering bullying, abuse, humiliation – privations that were to resurface vividly in Charlotte's *Jane Eyre* as Lowood School.

The School Register of the Clergy Daughter's School (1825) has this to say about three of the Brontë schoolchildren:

> *Charlotte Brontë* [age 8] entered Aug 10 1824. Writes indifferently. Ciphers a little, and works neatly. Knows nothing about grammar, geography, history or accomplishments. Altogether above average but knows nothing systematically. Left school June 1 1825. Governess.
>
> *Marie Brontë*. Aged 10 July 1 1824. Reads tolerably. Writes pretty well. Ciphers a little. Works badly. Has made some progress in reading French but knows nothing of the language grammatics … died May 16, 1825.
>
> *Emily Brontë*. Entered November 25 1824 age 5¾. Reads very prettily and works a little.

Patrick Brontë took the perpetual curacy of St Michael and All Angels' Church in Haworth. He wrote of his appointment in 1820: 'My salary is not large; it is only about £200 a year. I have a good house, which is mine also, and is rent-free'. His parish, too, had something of a reputation: in 1672 the Rev. Oliver Heywood had put it about that Haworth was 'a very immoral and profane place'. Presumably, by the time Patrick arrived this damning calumny was a thing of the past.

Maria developed ovarian cancer after moving to Haworth and died a painful death on 15 September 1821. Anne Brontë, her youngest daughter, was only twenty months old at the time.

Elizabeth Gaskell did Patrick Brontë no favours when she described him in her biography of Charlotte as a 'strange' and 'half-mad' man who was 'not naturally fond of children', a description that has endured ever since it was published in 1857. She goes on to say he saw 'their [the children's] frequent appearance as a drag both on his wife's strength, and as interruption to the comfort of the household'. Moreover, he was prone to fits of violent temper that included burning his children's boots, shredding his wife's gown and firing a gun out the kitchen door; Gaskell also says that he would make his daughters wear masks while he questioned them about moral issues, which he insisted would 'make them speak with less timidity'. Brontë's own description of the practice is no less alarming but it does show that he did it with the best of intentions: the eldest was about ten and the youngest four and his aim was for them to 'stand and speak boldly', 'to make them speak with less timidity' because he suspected they knew more than they each let on.

If a counterbalance to Gaskell's description of Brontë were required then we need go no further than Dudley Green's *Patrick Brontë: Father of Genius* (2010), in which the author 'aims to rehabilitate a man misunderstood and maligned by the Brontë myth since Mrs Gaskell'. But in contrast to Gaskell's portrayal of Patrick as 'a remote father given to eccentric behaviour and strange fits of passion', Green, like the servant quoted above, believes him to have been a kind and devoted parent with 'a keen interest in his children's development and an able and faithful clergyman, who was ever sensitive to the pastoral needs of his parishioners'.

The paradox of the man is clearly illustrated by the contrast between his own moralistic writings and the liberal, wide-ranging literary diet he prescribed for his children. On the one hand we have *The Phenomenon; or, an Account in verse of the extraordinary disruption of a bog, which took place in the moors of Haworth, on the 12th day of September, 1824.* The Phenomenon was designed to be a reward for children who excelled in their Sunday school classes; the preface thunders out:

> If you read the Scriptures and other good books only, your souls will be edified and comforted; but if you read every tract that is put into your hands by cunning and designing people, or eagerly search out for, and peruse such tracts and books as you know before to be bad, then you are sure to be corrupted and misled, and your talent of reading will become a source of sin and misery to yourselves and others.

On the other hand, it comes as some relief when we learn from Christine Alexander in the *Oxford Dictionary of National Biography* that:

> Unlike most middle-class Victorian households, there was little censorship of reading in the Brontë parsonage. The Bible was staple fare; yet Patrick Brontë also encouraged an eclectic diet of Homer, Virgil, Shakespeare, Bunyan, Milton, Pope, Johnson, Gibbon, Cowper, Burns, Wordsworth, Coleridge, Scott, Southey, and Byron ...

Brontë was a formidable, unforgiving preacher, demanding attention at all times when he was in the pulpit: his sexton was armed with a long staff and patrolled the aisles 'knobbing' sleepers and throwing threatening glances at misbehaving children.

However, despite their father's best efforts to maximise educational opportunities for the surviving girls, they were always going to be constricted by the societal norms that dictated the course of middle class women's lives: their only options were marriage, or careers as a school mistress or governess. Of the three, only Emily never became a governess; she had a short spell teaching in Miss Patchett's school at Law Hill between Haworth and Halifax. Charlotte had teaching positions at Miss Margaret Wooler's school, and in Brussels with the Hegers. She became governess to the Sidgwicks, the Stonegappes and the Lotherdales, then with Mrs White, at Upperhouse House, Rawdon, in 1841. Anne worked as governess for Mrs Ingham at Blake Hall, Mirfield, in 1839, then for Mrs Robinson at Thorp Green Hall, Little Ouseburn, near York.

'The Life & Age of Woman – Stages of Woman's Life from the Cradle to the Grave', a 1849 US print illustrating eleven chronological prescribed stages of virtuous womanhood (with the 30s evidently considered to be the peak years), each accompanied by a descriptive verse couplet. At left is a flourishing green tree, at right a symbolic weeping willow. Here is an approximate transcription of the verse couplets: 1) Infant in cradle; 2) Young girl with doll; 3) Late teen girl in grownup clothes; 4) Bride in white dress and veil; 5) Young mother holding baby; 6) Dressed to go outdoors (i.e. now that she no longer has babies or toddlers in the house, she can now take an interest in matters outside the home — though in a strictly private and individual charitable capacity, of course); 7) Middle-aged woman (first declining step): 'Absorbed in household duties now, The weight of toil(?) contracts her brow.'; 8) In black bonnet and holding handkerchief (suggesting the latter stages of mourning, perhaps her husband has died); 9) Old, wearing spectacles; 10) Bent over, using cane; 11) Sitting in chair, knitting(?): 'The body sinks and wastes away, The spirit cannot know dismay.'(?) Vignette under arch: Funeral scene. Edited from image http://memory.loc.gov/master/pnp/cph/3 g00000/3g03000/3g03600/3g03651u.tif at the Library of Congress website.

Elizabeth Gaskell reveals in her *Life of Charlotte Brontë* [p. 123] that Robert Southey, poet laureate, told Charlotte that ladies from a good background should be content with an education and a marriage embellished with some decorative talents. It is doubtful that this advice would have rested well with Charlotte. It is hard, too, to reconcile Patrick Brontë's relatively enlightened approach to his girls' education and careers with the statement by one of the characters in his *The Maid of Kilarney*:

> The education of female ought, most assuredly, to be competent, in order that she might enjoy herself, and be a fit companion for man. But, believe me, lovely, delicate and sprightly woman, is not formed by nature, to

pore over the musty pages of Grecian and Roman literature, or to plod through the windings of Mathematical Problems, nor has Providence assigned for her sphere of action, either the cabinet or the field. Her forte is softness, tenderness and grace.

In any case, it seemed to contradict his attitude towards his daughters whom he encouraged even if he was not completely aware of what they did with their time.

The literary and artistic influences on the three girls were many and various, and included Byron and John Martin, the Romantic painter (1789–1854). Charlotte and Branwell worked together on copies of the prints *Belshazzar's Feast*, *Déluge*, and *Joshua Commanding the Sun to Stand Still upon Gibeon* (1816), which their father hung on the walls of the parsonage.

In 1846, Patrick Brontë went to Manchester with Charlotte, to have cataract surgery – an operation performed without anaesthetic. At the time, ophthalmic surgeons had not mastered the use of stitches to hold the incision in the eye together: consequently, Brontë had to lie quietly recuperating in a darkened room for some weeks after the operation. Charlotte used her time to begin work on *Jane Eyre*.

As a widower, in 1847 Patrick campaigned for improved education in the district; he was responsible for building a Sunday school in Haworth, the National School Sunday school that opened in 1832. Crucially, between 1849 and 1850 he put in place plans for a clean water supply for the village, which came to fruition in 1856. He also campaigned vigorously against campaigning against the injustices of the Poor laws, and closed the local whist shops.

After Charlotte's death, Patrick Brontë co-operated with Elizabeth Gaskell on her biography of his last surviving child. He also arranged for the posthumous publication of Charlotte's first novel, *The Professor*, in 1857. Tragically, Brontë outlived not only his wife by forty years but all six of his children.

Speaking to D. Davies the Rev. Brontë commented on the vexed question of the recently published biography of Charlotte Brontë: 'It is full of lies,' he said; 'but since it appears to amuse the public it is of no importance to me' [D. Davies (1896) 'Haworth Thirty-Seven Years Ago', *Temple Bar and London Magazine for Town and Country Readers* 107, 132–9]. This was in allusion to the disparaging stories told about himself.

MR CHARLOTTE BRONTË

'that wicked man who was the death of dear Charlotte'

Charlotte Brontë said of Arthur Bell Nicholls in her letters that he looked to be a respectable young man who read well, and she hoped that he would 'give satisfaction'. He regularly visited the parish poor but was seen as being strict and formal; for example, in 1847 he ran a very unpopular (and mean-spirited) campaign to stop women from hanging their washing out to dry. Titus Salt over in Saltaire had demonstrated similar antipathy there. Indeed, Charlotte was sad to report that while he was away on holiday in Ireland many parishioners hoped he would not return. In December 1848 he conducted the funeral service of Emily Brontë.

A Simon Palmer watercolour that neatly captures
Salt's dislike of the public display of washing, and a
remorseful housewife, after being rebuked by Salt.

When, on 13 December 1852, Nicholls asked Charlotte for her hand in marriage, Charlotte's father was apoplectic: his somewhat un-Christian reason being that a poor Irish pastor should never have the temerity to marry his famous daughter, obviously forgetting that he, too, was Irish and had once been poor and a pastor to boot. Brontë dismissed Nicholls as 'an unmanly driveller'. The next year, Nicholls gave up his ambition on Charlotte and decided to leave the village, but later had second thoughts even though a self-interested Patrick Brontë had given him a reference and the (soon to be disappointed) parishioners had provided a leaving present. Several clandestine meetings with Charlotte in Haworth followed as her resistance gradually eroded and in February 1854 her father finally gave in and gave permission for him to visit her. Arthur Nicholls married Charlotte Brontë on 29 June 1854 in her father's church but Patrick Brontë stayed away; his daughter was escorted up the aisle by Margaret Wooler, Charlotte's former schoolmistress at Roe Head School. The couple honeymooned in Wales and Ireland before returning to live with Charlotte's father and her sisters at Haworth Parsonage. On their return, tea and supper for about five hundred were given in the schoolroom.

Nine months later, Charlotte died suddenly. Nicholls proved a difficult and prickly copyright holder of her works in the face of the explosion of interest in Charlotte, which started with the pseudonymous publication of *Jane Eyre* in 1847 and the public exposure of her real, female, identity in 1850. It all came to a head in the months after the announcement of her death and the Brontë myth began to take shape. In a bid to correct the skewed impressions the public were formulating about Charlotte's private life fuelled by an ever sensationalist press, Patrick Brontë called on Charlotte's friend, novelist Elizabeth Gaskell, to put things right with an authorised biography and stifle the Brontë mythology that was proliferating.

Arthur Nicholls did not want to sanction this, especially as it would allow Gaskell access to Charlotte's personal correspondence. He relented but when *The Life of Charlotte Brontë* was published in 1857 he became obsessive, penning vociferous letters to national newspapers, defending Gaskell's descriptions of Charlotte Brontë's wretched school days against her teachers who now felt they had been slandered. The book was withdrawn and re-issued twice with amendments, but the expurgations did little more than inflame the public's imagination. Patrick Brontë was at first happy with the book but later he expressed reservations relating to what he considered to be an unfair portrayal of Nicholls, based as it was largely on the opinion of disaffected Ellen Nussey.

Jane Eyre and the public outrage demonstrated by Nicholls contributed to the frenzy: the parsonage became a place of pilgrimage for admirers and the short walk down to the church had to be negotiated with care as Brontë and Nicholls were forced to push their way through the crowds of people wanting to touch the cape of the father of the Brontë sisters. Hundreds, thousands even thronged the village; a torrent that has continued apace ever since: the parsonage remains one of the most visited literary sites in the world.

The parsonage in snow, 27 February 2018. © Mark Davis

The widowed Nicholls stayed at Haworth Parsonage as Patrick's assistant until Brontë's death in June 1861; the natural progression was for Nicholls to succeed him but the church trustees were unenthusiastic and voted him down; he resigned and auctioned off the contents of Haworth Parsonage, retaining only the Brontë sisters' manuscripts and private effects before moving back to Ireland.

Indeed, it seems that Nicholls had few friends: Ellen Nussey, Charlotte's friend, was particularly excoriating, describing him as 'that wicked man who was the death of dear Charlotte'. According to Elizabeth Gaskell, he was intransigent and bigoted, adding in qualification that Charlotte, however, 'would never have been happy but with an exacting, rigid, law-giving, passionate man'. On the other hand, the two servants at the parsonage Tabitha Aykroyd and Martha Brown, believed that Charlotte and Arthur were happy together.

To add to the controversy, on Boxing Day 1854 Charlotte wrote that Arthur 'is certainly my dear boy, and he is dearer to me today than he was six months ago'.

THE PARSONAGE AND THE BRONTË SOCIETY, 1893

The parsonage through the graveyard, 27 February 2018. © Mark Davis

To many people, Haworth is synonymous with the parsonage, and the parsonage is synonymous with Haworth. In 1928, Sir James Roberts, a lifelong Brontë Society member, acquired the house for £3,000, equipped it as a museum and gifted it to The Brontë Society when it became a museum. Roberts (1848–1935) was a typical local man born at Lane Ends, near Haworth, one of eleven children of a weaver who became a tenant farmer. He knew Charlotte Brontë and heard her father preach, graduating from school at eleven to become a part-time millworker in Oxenhope; two years later he was apprenticed at William Greenwood's mill there. At the age of eighteen he became manager of the mill, and in 1873 he set up his own business as a top-maker (top-making prepares the wool for the spinning process, at which the wool is formed into a yarn). Later in life Sir James Roberts bought Salts Mill from the family of the founder, Sir Titus Salt, saving it from bankruptcy. T.S. Eliot, an acquaintance, references Roberts in *The Waste Land* as 'a silk hat on a Bradford millionaire'.

Glimpses into the parsonage © Mark Davis

Homely as it may have been on the inside, the parsonage on the outside was at the mercy of the inclement elements as the winds battered down from the moors: Elizabeth describes it: 'on autumnal or winter nights, the four winds of heaven seemed to meet and rage together, tearing round the house as if they were wild beasts trying to find an entrance' [p. 49].

The blasted moor in 2009 © Mark Davis

The Brontë Society has presided over a number of refurbishments, the latest of which was completed in 2013. This includes the result of a two-year research programme conducted by the University of Lincoln, wallpaper expert Allyson McDermott and Ann Dinsdale, the Society's Principal Curator.

In 2013 the house was faithfully redecorated using contemporary descriptions, surviving invoices and accounts, sampling and cross-section evidence to achieve an authentic reconstruction of how it would have appeared in the 1850s. The wallpapers are either exact replicas or contemporary patterns and colours known to have been popular at the time. Most of the furniture is from when the Brontës lived in the house, collected by the Brontë Society from the 1890s.

An estate agent today would describe it something like this:

> The parsonage was originally known as the Glebe House, built in 1778–1779. A five-bay, stone and purpose-built clergy residence, with a fine doorcase, it is not more distinguished than many a farmhouse or land-agent's house, but it sits at the head of the village.

Elizabeth Gaskell, in her *The Life of Charlotte Bronte* in 1857 adds detail: she tells us that it was an oblong stone house, facing down the hill on which the village stands and with the front door right opposite to the western door of the church, about a hundred yards away. Of this space twenty yards or so in depth are occupied by the grassy garden. The house comprises four rooms on each floor, and is two storeys high. When the Brontës moved in, they made the larger parlour, to the left of the entrance, the family sitting room, while that on the right was procured by Mr Brontë as a study. Behind this was the kitchen, and behind the former, a sort of flagged storeroom. Upstairs, there were four bedrooms of similar size.

To Gaskell this was the epitome of an English country parsonage, as lived in by a family of very moderate means …

> Everything about the place tells of the most dainty order, the most exquisite cleanliness. The door-steps are spotless; the small old fashioned window-panes glitter like looking glasses.

Gaskell highlights the significant dichotomy between the 'pestiferous' infernal gloom exuded from the churchyard next door, with the homely domesticity radiated inside house itself with fires emitting a 'pretty warm dancing light all over the house'.

Like Gaskell, pilgrims, aficionados, scholars and students alike rightly regard the parsonage as everything the Brontë experience should be; entirely fitting for a house that had been a hotbed of literary creativity without peer.

The sisters' writing, of course, resulted in a significant demand for writing materials locally: this anecdote reported by Turner (p. 90) makes interesting reading:

> John Greenwood supplied them with stationery. He gave the following outline of his transactions with the sisters. 'About 1848, I began to do a

little in the stationery line. Nothing of that kind could be had nearer than Keighley before I began. They used to buy a great deal of writing paper, and I used to wonder whatever they did with so much. I sometimes thought they contributed to the magazines. When I was out of stock, I was always afraid of their coming; they seemed so distressed about it, if I had none.'

Further details regarding the meticulous and science-based redecoration of the parsonage are that the hallway, staircase hall and landing have been repainted a pale blue-grey established by paint analysis; Ellen Nussey, described it as 'a pretty dove-coloured tint'. Patrick's study had no such frippery: his austere study had never seen a roll of wallpaper and is accordingly repainted white.

Mrs Gaskell tells how 'the parlour has evidently been refurbished with within the last few years … The prevailing colour of the room is crimson'. Charlotte ordered red curtains woven in crimson 'union cloth' and a hand-printed paper in contemporary design, in a crimson trellis pattern against a white background. The Rev. Brontë detested curtains.

With her wedding imminent the stone-flagged storeroom was converted into a study by Charlotte for her fiancé, Arthur Nicholls. She wrote: 'I have been very busy stitching; the new little room is got into order, and the green and white curtains are up; they exactly suit the paper, and look neat and clean enough.' It is amazing to record that a scrap of wallpaper from this room was found in the New York Public Library with an authentication by Gaskell. Using this, the wallpaper has been re-created, as have curtains of a diligently researched contemporary and complementary design. The pattern was printed onto original nineteenth-century linen.

An 1850s wallpaper design chosen in a green colour evidenced from surviving paint fragments now graces Patrick's bedroom. Branwell's studio has been re-papered with an exact reproduction of a surviving scrap and Charlotte's room has been repainted a blue-green colour.

The Brontë Society was founded in 1893, and continues to extend the collection of 'Brontëana', which now includes around 7,000 objects.

On Patrick Brontë's death in 1861 a handwritten auction sale catalogue featuring furniture and household goods was issued, resulting in the sale of many pieces locally, pieces that remained in the hands of local families. Over time the auctioned goods found their way back to the parsonage and were complemented by memorabilia and correspondence from friends and servants. In 1893, the chief librarian of Bradford Library suggested that relics, letters and documents relating to the Brontës should all be collected and preserved for posterity. This led to the foundation of The Brontë Society at a public meeting where a collection of Brontëana was started. By 1895 the collection had grown large enough to be displayed in a museum opened above the Yorkshire Penny Bank in Haworth Main Street. The society attracted 260 members, with about 10,000 visitors visiting the museum in its inaugural year. Henry Houston Bonnell, a wealthy Philadelphia publisher, bequeathed his extensive collection of Brontë manuscripts, letters, first editions and personal effects, which arrived at the Museum when he died in 1926. The mahogany desk at which Charlotte wrote her novels, and had been in private hands for more than a century, was donated to the museum; the anonymous donor had purchased it for £20,000 in 2009.

Today, the society has about 1,800 members.

Rewriting *Wuthering Heights*

2017 saw the beginning of a wonderful project at the Parsonage Museum that involved handwriting all thirty-four chapters of *Wuthering Heights* by no fewer than 10,000 visitors. The original manuscript no longer survives, so these ten thousand visitors were invited to copy one line from the novel in their own hand into a handmade book to be exhibited from 17 February 2018, Emily Brontë's bicentenary year.

Clare Twomey, a British artist and a research fellow at the University of Westminster, is in charge of the project. Each 'author' has been gifted a pencil, commissioned by the artist, as a tool with which to keep on writing. The hope is that the unique act of sitting at a table in the house where Emily wrote her novel, and to hold a pencil and write, 'will build understanding of Emily and her determination to create the one published work of her lifetime'.

BRANWELL BRONTË

The man who painted himself out of his own family

Given the celebrity and talent enjoyed by his three surviving sisters, the fact that Patrick Branwell Brontë (1817–1848) was considered by his father and those very sisters to be a genius makes him all the more remarkable. Destined for ever to be in the shadow of Emily, Charlotte and Anne, Branwell is further benighted by his gradual decline at the mercy of addictions to laudanum and alcohol. However, before this, he was obviously a clever, gifted and inspirational son and brother and was the driving force behind the vivid and imaginary worlds his sisters contrived and with which they launched their nascent literary careers. The sextant who succeeded Arthur Bell Nicholls, a man named Wade, remembered:

> seeing Branwell sitting in the vestry, talking to his (the sexton's) father, and writing two different letters at the same time. He could take a pen in each hand, and write a letter with each at once.
>
> ['A Winter-Day at Haworth' *Chambers's Journal*.
> 4th ser. no. 217 (22 Feb. 1868), 124–128]

Some have even speculated that they see the hand of Branwell in his sisters' work – a 'Branwellian' school, which since the 1920s at least, is convinced that he actually wrote *Wuthering Heights*, and more of the Brontë books.

It is a theory that has attracted derision, and which was fabulously satirised in Stella Gibbons' 1932 *Cold Comfort Farm*, in which the character Mr Mybug is busy writing a book on the conspiracy theory. Mr Mybug knows best: 'You see, it's obvious that it's his book and not Emily's. No woman could have written that. It's male stuff …'

Branwell's route to the Black Bull and the apothecary from the parsonage.
The snow scene clearly shows the old Apothecary, taken
on 27 February 2018. 055/A © Mark Davis

Home-educated by his father and tutors, the plan was for Branwell to embark on
a career as a tutor, to which end in January 1840, he started his employment with
the family of Robert Postlethwaite in Broughton-in-Furness. Branwell obviously
missed his hedonistic Haworth social life because he wrote letters to his fellow
drinkers in Haworth which, according to his entry in the *Brontë Encyclopedia*, give
'a vivid picture of Branwell's scabrous humour, his boastfulness, and his need to
be accepted in a man's world'. We also learn that he celebrated his new job with
a bacchanalian night out in Kendal.

Four early photographs of the Black Bull, one of the scenes of
Branwell's decline. Note the stocks. © Mark Davis

Attempts to succeed as an artist just led to a prodigal trip to London with Branwell
consorting in various dens of iniquity, while Anne's attempts to keep him on the
straight and narrow by finding work for him in January 1843 at Thorp Green Hall,
Little Ouseburn, near York, where he was tutor to the Reverend Edmund Robinson's
son, ended after three years when he was dismissed. There is controversy still over
why but it seems likely that it involved Mrs Robinson and the two-year affair she
conducted with Branwell. Over 100 years later the lyrics to Simon and Garfunkel's
Mrs Robinson are apt: *It's a little secret, just the Robinsons' affair. Most of all, you've
got to hide it from the kids.* Indeed, Mrs Lydia Robinson inspired the name of the
character Mrs Robinson, who has an affair with an intelligent but confused young

man, in Charles Webb's novel *The Graduate* (1963) and the 1967 film of the same name. Back in the nineteenth century, Elizabeth Gaskell wrote to her publisher describing Mrs Robinson as 'that bad woman who corrupted Branwell Brontë'.

Branwell's legacy as an author includes *Juvenilia*, which he wrote as a child with Charlotte, *Glass Town* and *Angria*, poems and prose and verse under the pseudonym of Northangerland; *Real Rest* was published by the *Halifax Guardian* (8 November 1846); there is also an unfinished novel from around 1845 called *And the Weary are at Rest* based on *Angria*.

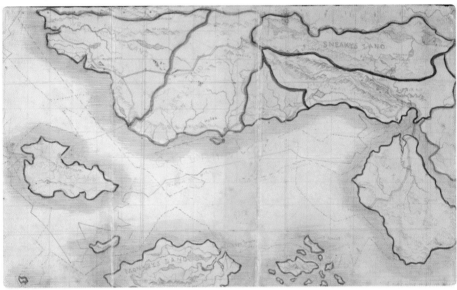

A hand-drawn map of the imaginary country of Angria from Branwell and Charlotte Brontë's notebooks, between 1830 and 1831. Manuscript of *The History of the Young Men from their First Settlement to the Present Time* (British Library shelfmark Ashley2468).

The downwards spiral continued with Branwell accidentally setting fire to his bed and notes to a friend asking for '5d worth of Gin'. Needless to say, the Temperance lobby had a field day at Branwell's expense, using the fame and celebrity of his sisters as a backdrop for his alcoholism. An example of the fire and brimstone comes with:

> Wonderful was the power of intellect which early developed itself and was common to all the family. Deep were the waters of bodily and mental sufferings through which they all had to pass, and one of the blackest shadows thrown over their lives, was one which darkens the lot of thousands whose day would otherwise be bright and blissful as Eden—a horrible shadow, and its name is DRINK.
>
> These sisters had an only brother who gave the same promise of intellectual excellence as themselves. The mantle of genius had fallen on the family, and Patrick Brannell Brontë [sic] gave early evidence of great mental power. His sisters predicted a brilliant course for him. They did not doubt that he would distinguish himself, and carve his name in large and legible letters,

on that fame-pillar ' whose towering summit ambient clouds conceal.' They fondly loved him, and with true sisterly affection, were willing to make any sacrifice for his advancement. Every loss—which promoted his interest, they would have counted gain. And who can tell how proud a name he might have won, had he not fallen a victim to intemperance? Very early was his soul tainted by this sin, and the taint spread and grew till his manliness was gone—till his mind was shattered, and his moral nature laid waste—till his conscience was a hell, his days madness, and his nights despair. The wit and talent of yo ... hitterly than for his early death. What a warning does this narrative give to young men. Here is character destroyed, a brilliant prospect o'erclouded, a glorious intellect shattered, a young life prematurely ended, and for the moral which this teaches we have not far to seek, nor is it hard to find, it is one which even he who runs may read, 'Beware of strong drink.' ... To tamper with it is perilous to all your interests, touch it not, taste it not, wholly abstain.

['OPQ' (1858) Brunnel Brontë: A Warning to Young Men,
The United Methodist Free Churches Magazine]

Nathaniel Currier (1813–1888) and James Merritt Ives (1824–1895) produced over thirty prints that focussed graphically on the Temperance Movement. This one shows a semi-circle of male figures beginning with Step 1. 'A glass with a Friend' up and over semi-circle to Step 9 'Death by suicide.' Half circle bottom centre with an image of a weeping woman walking with a child.
Steps: 1. A glass with a Friend 2. A glass to keep the cold out 3. A glass too much 4. Drunk and riotous 5. The Summit attained; Jolly Companions; a confirmed Drunkard 6. Poverty and Disease 7. Forsaken by Friends 8. Desperation and crime 9. Death by suicide'.

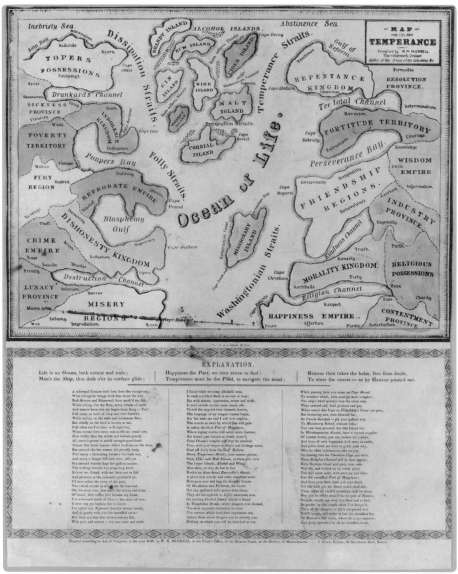

William Meacham Murrell's equally evocative 1846 Map of Temperance. The website tells us that it is 'An early allegorical map on temperance, accompanied by a lengthy poem. Typical of 'didactic' visual aids intended to be 'at once entertaining and instructive ... colorful and intricate temperance maps depicting the 'Ocean of Life' trained viewers to see that the path to damnation was ... a veritable riptide towing the sinner from the first sip of grog to the channel of destruction. The apparent innocuousness and swift danger of water made it a potent metaphor for life's temptations in an era when waterways were primary transportation routes, and accidental drownings and shipwrecks not uncommon. The maps vividly showed that 'Religion Channel' was just one strong current away from 'Misery Regions' and the 'Reprobate Empire,' not only for seasoned tipplers but for all on the 'Ocean of Life.''

The Black Bull from above

Indeed, if late nineteenth century accounts of visitors to Haworth are anything to go by, the pub is the cause of almost as much interest as the church and the parsonage itself. Take this rather pious account from 1876:

> Branwell Brontë entered [the parlour of the Black Bull] rather too often. 'A little red-haired, light-complexioned chap,' he was described to us, 'and a wonderful fellow for wit and learning. He could dictate four letters at once, as fast as ever you could write.' Our informant was an old man, whose name I forget, though he told us readily enough. 'He was cleverer, Branwell was, nor onny of his sisters, or all put together, and what they put i' their books, they got from him.' And as a proof of this wonderful cleverness, he pointed to an arm-Windsor-chair in which I was sitting, and said: 'Hey, mony's the times I've seen him i' that chair, talking away and astonishing everybody.' 'I suppose you knew him very well?' I said. 'Oh, ay; I've seen him in mony a scrape. What letters he used to write to me, to be sure, when he was from home a tutoring. He was oft fast for brass; and I used to help him a bit.'
>
> ['On the Yorkshire Hills about Haworth'. *Temple Bar* 19(1867), 428–432]

We find the same pub parlour ambience was recorded in an 1864 visit:

> Here also stands the Black-Bull tavern, famous as the place where Patrick Brontë, the son, — or Branwell, as he was called, — was wont to spend his evenings carousing with his old boon companions … In the room opposite the one where I sat, a dozen, perhaps, of the old villagers had assembled about the blazing hearth; and their ruddy looks and loud

102

voices, their evening tales and hearty laughter, and the fumes that scented the house through every hall and apartment, told only too plainly, that the Black Bull still enjoys the reputation it had of yore … Then we went into a rear-room where Branwell used to meet his bad companions, entertain them with his flashes of wit and genius, and indulge with them in riotous excesses.

[A.J. Putnam (1864) 'A Visit at Haworth',
The Monthly Religious Magazine 31, 41–46]

Branwell's famous chair in the Black Bull from which he held forth

Black Bull apart, Branwell must have found friends and solace, too, at the Lodge of the Three Graces Haworth, which was reformed on 15 September 1792, its first recorded meeting having been convened at the Black Bull on 7 July 1806. This was the venue until 1821 when they moved to rooms in Newell Hill, now Lodge Street. The three-storey house of William Wood, a joiner, who made furniture for the parsonage and the coffins for the Brontë family is also here.

Branwell Brontë had been proposed and accepted into the Masonic lodge at Lodge Street on 29 February 1836; on 6 April 1836 he was elevated to 'the sublime degree of Master Mason'. On 12 June 1837 he became secretary; the last time he attended a lodge meeting was in 1842.

The Masons were not the only manifestation of sobriety and responsibility in Branwell's back pages. Apart from being organist, secretary and junior warden at the Lodge, he was member of a boxing club, founder of the anti-Chartist Haworth Operative Conservative Party and, in the cruellest of ironies, secretary of Haworth Temperance Society.

PILGRIMAGE TO HAWORTH

> We no sooner reached the foot of the hill than we had to begin to mount again, over a narrow, rough stone-paved road; the horses' feet seemed to catch at boulders, as if climbing. When we reached the top of the village there was apparently no outlet, but we were directed to drive into an entry which just admitted the gig; we wound round in the entry and then saw the church close at hand, and we entered on the short lane which led to the parsonage gateway. Here Charlotte was waiting, having caught the sound of the approaching gig.

This is how Ellen Nussey described her first sight of Haworth on a visit to see her friend Charlotte Brontë in 1833. As such it is fairly typical of the countless descriptions written by the many literary pilgrims to the village. After the deaths of the three sisters, the road up to Haworth was, as noted, exceedingly well trodden and has become one of *the* literary pilgrimages, not just in the British Isles, but in the world. Today, Haworth is smart, tidy and buzzing and brimming with attractive shops, pubs and agreeable places to eat. But it was not always like this. The romantic, sentimental assumption for those people who have declined to scrape the surface (or indeed read any of the novels or poetry) is that Haworth was, since the Brontë era at least, an idyll, a nice, twee Yorkshire village – a place just right for those nice lady writers with their nice books; the sort of place you would see emblazoned on a tin of Bettys biscuits in close-by leafy Ilkley.

Not so. By common consent of those who did make the journey from the second half of the nineteenth century, Haworth was an 'ugly' place. Even taking into account the prevalent stereotypes – clichéd ruddy-faced natives with their 'grim up northness' that even today exposes the lazy stereotyper who writes off the 'gritty' north simply as a blasted heath above Haworth – even discounting this cant, the fine improvements you see today have taken place only in the last few decades. Back in the latter nineteenth century we hear a lot about clattering clogs, ruddy complexions and patronising descriptions of uneducated natives.

'The Clatter of Clogs in the Early Morning' by Fred Wilde in his
The Clatter of Clogs in the Early Morning (London, 1982)

Elizabeth Gaskell describes a visit to Haworth by neighbours of Charlotte Brontë
some time before 1857. We read of a journey past chimneys and mills through the
clouded moorland gloom where:

> the country got wilder and wilder as we approached Haworth; for the last
> four miles we were ascending a huge moor, at the very top of which lies
> the dreary black-looking village of Haworth. Open cast coal workings
> added to the industrial landscape. The village-street itself is one of the
> steepest hills I have ever seen.

[p. 344]

The parsonage was:

> a dreary, dreary place, literally *paved* with rain-blackened tombstones,
> and all on the slope ... here was an old man in the churchyard, brooding
> like a Ghoul over the graves, with a sort of grim hilarity on his face. I
> thought he looked hardly human ... presently a door opened [into the
> parlour] and in came a superannuated mastiff.

Even discounting the obvious Gothic hyperbole *Frankenstein*, *The Hounds of the
Baskervilles*, *Dracula* and *Tristram Shandy* all spring to mind.

The public relations and tourism industry were not well helped by Charlotte
Brontë, who repeatedly showed her scorn for the place. When just eighteen, she

described Haworth as 'only a miserable little village, buried in dreary moors and moss hags and marshes'. At age thirty-three in 1849, she advised her publisher before a visit by a member of staff that ' he will find Haworth a strange, uncivilised little place'; the following year Haworth was 'a remote district where education had made little progress' as described in her preface to Emily's *Wuthering Heights*. Her instructions to Elizabeth Gaskell before her visit were no less unflattering, and indeed her father was equally scathing in his description of the place. Charlotte, though, was not simply being haughty and superior: she may have had another agenda: to justify the vulgarity and crudeness that some of her critics levelled at her work, particularly *Jane Eyre*. Being seen to be writing from within such a social landscape would go some way to explaining the absence of Austen-like gentility in her work in much the same as the wild moors and the tempestuous weather might explain the physical landscape she and her sisters deployed.

Gaskell obviously agreed, firing off an early salvo in the eternal north-south divide controversy when she asserts in her biography:

> I have little doubt that in the every-day life of the people so independent, wilful, and full of grim humour, there would be much found even at present that would shock those only accustomed to the local manners of the south.

She added:

> Even now, a stranger can hardly ask a question without receiving some crusty reply, if, indeed, he receive any at all. Sometimes the sour rudeness amounts to positive insult. Yet, if the 'foreigner' takes all this churlishness good-humouredly, or as a matter of course, and makes good any claim upon their latent kindliness and hospitality, they are faithful and generous, and thoroughly to be relied upon.
>
> [Chapter 2]

Things got off badly for reality and accuracy: Matthew Arnold, the man who wrote of *Jane Eyre*:

> Miss Brontë has written a hideous, undelightful, convulsed, constricted novel … one of the most utterly disagreeable books I've ever read [because] the writer's mind contains nothing but hunger, rebellion and rage and therefore that is all she can, in fact, put in her book.

Arnold got it all wrong when he reburied Charlotte in a poem based on the supposition, despite the obvious evidence to the contrary, that Charlotte was buried in Haworth graveyard with her three sisters:

Haworth Churchyard, April, 1855

> How shall we honour the young,
> The ardent, the gifted? how mourn?   80
> Console we cannot; her ear

Is deaf. Far northward from here,
In a churchyard high mid the moors
Of Yorkshire, a little earth
Stops it for ever to praise.   85
Where, behind Keighley, the road
Up to the heart of the moors
Between heath-clad showery hills
Runs, and colliers' carts
Poach the deep ways coming down,   90
And a rough, grim'd race have their homes—
There, on its slope, is built
The moorland town. But the church
Stands on the crest of the hill,
Lonely and bleak; at its side   95
The parsonage-house and the graves.

Research at its worst.

But more objective, and accurate, views prevailed. In 1858, biographer William Scruton of the Bradford Historical & Antiquarian Society was only too pleased to find Charlotte's descriptions of Haworth to be quite wrong; having been taken in by the bad press pedalled by Miss Brontë and Mrs Gaskell, he jubilantly wrote 'we found all our expectations most gloriously disappointed … we found a large and flourishing village – not a very enlightened or poetical place certainly, but quaint, compact and progressive'.

A.J. Putnam describes his visit to Haworth in 1864, beginning with the trek from Keighley on which they pass:

> various scattered houses and factories on the way … [the] shops and houses seemed crowded with the necessaries and comfortables of life, and every thing indicated here a simple, frugal, hardy, happy people. Far up the hill, at the end of this long, rudely paved, and thickly populated street, is the centre, so to speak, of the town. Near it are the churches; and here are the two or three inns of the village; and here converge several of the compressed and irregular thoroughfares of the place.
>
> [A.J. Putnam (1864) 'A Visit at Haworth',
> *The Monthly Religious Magazine* 31, 41–46]

One year later, in 1865, J. Tomlinson also remarks on the industry around the village, 'all the way to Haworth, with a number of worsted mills to the right, situate in a deep narrow gorge, through which runs a little mountain stream, dignified by the name of river Worth'.

He struggles to get inside the psyche of the inhabitants, wondering whether the landscape and unforgiving weather holds the same thrilling fascination for them as it does the ardent Brontë pilgrim:

> I asked (mentally) what sort of people live in those cottages? Do they ever feel a thrill of joy on looking beyond these gentle slopes to the wild

grandeur of the distant hills? At one time the whole scene bursts out into new vigour with the rising sun; at other times a thick mist blends together the mountains and the clouds; while, in winter time, there are the huge white pyramids of snow. The people see all this year by year; but what do they feel? I cannot enter into the inner life of these rough cottagers; if, indeed, there lives anything there which is not purely mechanical ...

Tomlinson dispels any romanticism with a passing reference to the daily grind that is long hours of monotonous and hard work:

The labours of the day ended, groups of men and women, boys and girls, were lounging outside the dwellings, some squatted on the door-steps, others leaning against the walls. On passing two or three factory children, one of them stood still, stared full into my face and said, offering something which she had in her hand, 'Mon, a lugger.' Of course I took it, and thanked her, although it was nothing but a blade of grass: the bold familiarity of this girl I found to be a characteristic type of the people hereabout ...

To Tomlinson, the inhospitability of the place – and the apparently 'almost uncivilized population' put an end to any aspirations the Brontës had to setting up a school in Haworth:

the Misses Brontës were, for a long time, very anxious to open a small school at the parsonage, and even made their wishes known in quarters where they hoped for pupils: the situation and the place, however, proved an effectual barrier; no lady would send her daughters on to the wild moors, in the midst of a rough and almost uncivilized population: some other locality must be sought. Burlington was mentioned, then Leeds, when, unexpectedly, there came an offer from their old friend and teacher, Miss Wooler, of her establishment at Dewsbury Moor.

Their solution is at once highly enterprising and eminently sensible:

But before they set up school – keeping on their own account, the sisters thought it very desirable that they should become well grounded in French, Italian, German, at some continental school; this would give them a prestige in the eyes of the public. Accordingly Charlotte and Emily went to Brussels, the entire expense being defrayed by aunt Branwell.

Tomlinson does not spare us the harsh realities of northern hill farming life:

Alas! It is difficult to become enthusiastic when the sloppy, plashy ground and drizzling rain brings such discomfort. Before us are a number of tall calves, lean and ill-favoured as the kine which troubled Pharoah. Poor, prematurely-aged looking beasts, to you life can have little pleasure, with so very little to eat! Here are, also, some scraggy, clipped sheep, with black faces and long cow-tails. Now, even lean sheep, when clothed, are fit to be seen; but an old ewe or tup denuded of wool, with long thin neck and hollow flanks, is a truly hideous spectacle: and such are these.

But it is not all miserable, scraggy windswept sheep; a hint of a romantic picture finally intrudes:

> Further we go and more romantic the landscape becomes. Tall, jutting ridges there are almost barren of vegetation, and dusky hollows quite choked up with heather. In one direction the moor-land sweeps onward to the horizon, without revealing a single pathway or human habitation; while, on the other side, yonder precipitous road seems like a narrow tract to the other hemisphere.
>
> [Tomlinson, J. (1865) 'Haworth, where the Brontës Lived', *Some interesting Yorkshire Scenes,* London, 116–154]

In January 1867, W.H. Cooke, following in Gaskell's footsteps, was more reverential: to Cooke, Haworth was a place 'made sacred through the habitual presence of these gifted beings'. To him, the parsonage was 'almost consecrated ground' [W.H. Cooke, A Winter Day at Haworth, *St James's Magazine*].

Cooke confirms the place as a busy, bustling moorland village complete with steep street and higgledy-piggledy houses:

> I was standing at the head of a steep descent when I got this my first peep at Haworth. The road at my feet ran down the hill to a little stone bridge, crossed it, and then began to climb the hill that rose directly in front of me. But just at the point where it left the bridge, it suddenly became no longer a country road, passing between scanty fields and barren pieces of moorland, but a steep and crowded street. The houses, strangely unequal in size, but all alike in the bareness and vulgarity of their architecture, were crowded together as compactly as though the land on which they were built was in the heart of London, instead of on the side of a Yorkshire hill. From where I looked down upon them, the opposite sides of the way seemed so near as scarcely to leave room for a foot-passenger, and the street rose at such an angle that it seemed impossible that any animal less surefooted than a mule could traverse it.

Despite appearances, though, the village was deserted, presumably because our visitor had turned up on a Sunday, in between church services, giving Haworth a ghostly, Gothic ambience languishing in its state of industrial decline:

> There was little life visible in the village itself as I toiled up the steep flagged street. Many of the houses were closed. Hard times, such as we read of in Shirley, had come upon the people. The mills were silent, and the active 'hands' had sought employment elsewhere; so, scarcely a woman or child came out to watch me as I went up the road that led to Charlotte Brontë's home ... for the whole place seemed haunted with the faces and forms of those to whom this 'long, unlovely street' had once been so familiar ...
>
> ['A Winter-Day at Haworth' [1867]. *Chambers's Journal.* 4th ser. no. 217 (22 Feb. 1868), 124–128]

Also in 1867, another visitor remarked just how isolated Haworth was from the outside world, and not just to southern pilgrims but to close neighbours:

> On my first visit, I walked from Bradford, and, when well out of the town, I made a point of asking from everybody I met which was the way to Haworth, and how far it was? One good woman, who stood washing just inside the door, and couldn't stretch out her arm by reason of having both elbows in the suds, imparted to me the cheering intelligence that she 'didn't exactly know where it wor, but her father and muther wor wed theer, between thirty and forty year sin'.

Patience and persistence, however, are amply rewarded; despite the snotty-nosed urchins, the determined pilgrim is rewarded with an industrious, honest place with good people at its heart:

> From Keighley as from Bradford, Haworth lies in different directions, and at different distances, according to the individual of whom you ask information; and it is only when you get there that common consent permits it to be where it is … Everything you see is, in some sort, sacred to you. The distant hills, the stone wall skirting the road; the broad flagstones in front of the houses, which at this season are being copiously swilled and vigorously scrubbed; the beck down to your right; the mills; the chapels; the numerous children (would to goodness their noses were cleaner!); the women, baking, brewing, washing, scolding; the men, who meet your look with a clear, steady, intelligent, humorous eye; who are, you can't but think, honest, independent, not to be put upon, a little brusque, but not surly or impertinent, and with a deal of real courtesy at bottom. All these things are the things which Charlotte Brontë saw, and of which she has written. As you walk on, her spirit is always with you …

The answer to it all lies in its unique creation story:

> Haworth is the queerest place one can go to. The country-folk say it was made on a Saturday night. There was a little rubbish left after the creation, and Haworth was made out of that … An ugly place made glorious by the genius of a little woman.
>
> ['On the Yorkshire Hills about Haworth'.
Temple Bar 19 (1867), 428–432]

In an 1881 article entitled *'Charlotte Brontë', Girls and their Ways: A Book for and about Girls by One who knows them'* (pp. 287–294), the author takes no prisoners when (s)he archly describes Haworth as 'not a picturesque village, nor is its immediate neighbourhood picturesque'. (S)he does, however, concede that 'the landscapes beyond have a romance of form and colouring which probably had an influence upon the development of Charlotte Brontë's genius'.

L.B. Walford's 'The Home of Charlotte Brontë', written in 1890, brings us more grim reality with those clattering clogs and lusty urchins in a life lived in a desert of social and scenic monotony and isolation:

At last I was at Haworth—bleak, rude, grim Haworth; Haworth, within whose rough-hewn boundaries was lived out that strange, isolated family life, so monotonous and uneventful outwardly, so charged with passion and intensity within, which has made the hitherto unknown little village among the hills famous for evermore … Upon leaving the platform of a small, primitive station we mounted the steep and narrow little street—(it might have been the original of Bunyan's Pilgrim's Hill called Straight)— and steeper and steeper it rose in front of us at every step; while down its centre there presently poured, with a clatter, clatter, clatter of wooden clogs, the village lads and lasses just let loose from school, each lusty urchin clad in such a suit of brown corduroys as must have set at nought the rudest blasts of winter, to say nothing of rugged walls and gnarled branches.

[Walford, L. B. (1890) 'The Home of Charlotte Brontë', *Longman's Magazine* XV: LXXXVII 306–313]

Six years later and we have more of much the same, not least the clattering clogs of the mill workers, ruddy complexions but surprisingly civilised children:

I remember how my mind and imagination were at that time excited in the anticipation of an introduction into the magic realm of those wondrous creations which had so fascinated me with the glamour of their weird power. The clattering of the clogs of the mill-hands—men, women and children—in the streets at an early hour of the morning seemed even to be the prelude of the drama of Hollow's Mill, narrated in 'Shirley' with so much graphic force and tragic circumstance …

The village was, however, not without its bizarre eccentricities, one of which was the spectacle of a three-legged dog scaling a ladder.

upreared against one of the houses, to rejoin his master who was labouring upon the roof. The care and ingenuity of the animal in planting his paws upon the rungs surprised us, as he had only the use of three legs. One was struck by the solid manner in which these houses were for the most part built. They were of sandstone, with mullioned windows having pointed or rounded arches. The interiors were seen in passing to be perfectly clean and well ordered. The children were mostly of a ruddy complexion, had light or red hair, and a more cultivated manner and look than one would have expected to find there.

The village of Haworth at that time consisted of a single street precipitously steep, surmounted by the church, the parsonage, and the 'Black Bull Inn.' The parsonage was a bare, stone, squarely-built house'.

[D. Davies (1896) 'Haworth Thirty-Seven Years Ago', *Temple Bar and London Magazine for Town and Country Readers* 107, 132–139]

The writer goes on to describe the parsonage as 'ugly, not at all like the picturesque tenement vignetted in Mrs G's book'.

THE BRONTË LANDSCAPE*

A landscape ceases to be topographical when there are people in it. When those people are the Brontë sisters, the landscape is far more than topographical. It becomes a literary landscape, but the literature cannot be fully appreciated without the topography, nor in the case of these sisters, something of their biography the Brontë novels are redolent of the moors that roll away from the bleak upland manufacturing village of Haworth.

[Arthur Pollard, Preface to *The Landscape of the Brontës*]

Countless books and articles have been written about landscape in the novels and poetry of the three Brontë sisters – and rightly so: the use of landscape in the Brontë oeuvres defines those books and their characters, and remains one of the reasons why they have enjoyed a universal appeal since publication.

Of course, early readers immediately recognised the importance of the local landscape of the moors, rather than the local community, to all three novelists. This from Elizabeth Gaskell:

From their first going to Haworth, their walks were directed rather out towards the heathery moors, sloping upwards behind the parsonage, than towards the long descending village street … at that time the six little creatures used to walk out, hand in hand, towards the glorious wild moors, which in after days they loved so passionately; the elder ones taking thoughtful care for the toddling wee things.

[Chapter 3; p. 40]

Indeed, Charlotte calls this landscape the 'wild workshop' in her Biographical Notice to the 1850 edition of Emily's *Wuthering Heights*.

Charlotte Brontë (1816–1855)

Landscape is integral to the Brontë sisters themselves – it is in their DNA. As a young woman Charlotte went to work at Roe Head School between 1831 and 1832 and, even though away from Haworth, still reminisced on the Haworth landscape when, homesick, she heard the wind blow at Roe Head; it was the Haworth wind that was blowing:

---

* This chapter is adapted in part from the Brontë chapters in my *Yorkshire Literary Landscapes*.

> The wind pouring in impetuous current through the air, sounding wildly, unremittingly from hour to hour, deepening its tone as the night advances, coming not in gusts, but with a rapid gathering stormy swell. That wind I know is heard at this moment far away on the moors at Haworth. Branwell and Emily hear it, as it sweeps over our house, down the Churchyard and round the old church, they think perhaps of me and Anne.

And, as noted, it's not just the wind, it's the whole landscape that immerses and imbues. Charlotte writes in 1850:

> My sister Emily had a particular love for them [the moors], and there is not a knoll of heather, not a branch of fern, not a young bilberry leaf not a fluttering lark or linnet but reminds me of her. The distant prospects were Anne's delight, and when I look round, she is in the blue tints, the pale mists, the waves and shadows of the horizon. In the hill-country silence their poetry comes by lines and stanzas into my mind.

But it was not always fond memories of a Haworth heaven on earth. The following rather contradicts what Charlotte had written in the very same *Roe Head Journal* of 1831–1832 when describing Haworth, showing just how homesickness and time can dictate one's feelings and inject a dose of realism:

> no other landscape than a monotonous street – of moorland, a grey church tower, rising from the centre of a graveyard so filled with graves that the rank weed and coarse grass scarce had room to shoot up between the monuments.

Sentiments that we revisit in her preface to her sister Emily's *Wuthering Heights*, wondering why the complete strangers in the burgeoning tourist trade they had created had any interest in the 'wild moors of northern England'. Indeed, Elizabeth Gaskell concurred with these bleak comments on the bleak landscape when she wrote in her *Life of Charlotte Brontë* after an early autumn visit:

> It was a dull, drizzly Indian-inky day ... lead coloured [passing] grey, dull-coloured rows of stone cottages ... poor, hungry-looking fields; stone fences everywhere, and trees nowhere ... moors everywhere above and beyond.

Emily Brontë (1818–1848)

Emily Brontë taught at Miss Patchett Ladies' Academy at Law House, near Halifax, for six months in 1837–1838. She later used her experiences here as a source for parts of her only novel, *Wuthering Heights* (1847), published under the pseudonym Ellis Bell. If Dante Gabriel Rossetti is to be believed, the landscape created by Emily is nothing short of chthonic: 'A fiend of a book – an incredible monster [...] The action is laid in hell, – only it seems places and people have English names there'. While maybe not quite hell on earth, wild, bleak and desolate the setting for *Wuthering Heights* certainly is, and Brontë has drawn for us one of the greatest, most vivid landscapes in English literature, made all the more atmospheric and dramatic because it was there, all around and enveloping her, tangible, dynamic and visible on her very doorstep at the Haworth parsonage.

In a letter to George Henry Lewes, philosopher, literary and theatre critic and partner of Mary Ann Evans (George Eliot) Charlotte Brontë criticised Jane Austen's fiction for depicting a restricted (and restricting) nineteenth-century equivalent of twenty-first-century tidy and manicured suburbia: 'carefully-fenced, highly cultivated garden, with neat borders and delicate flowers … a highly-cultivated garden and no open country'. The landscape we encounter in *Wuthering Heights* could not be further removed. 'Nature', as Professor John Bowen points out in his *Walking the Landscape of Wuthering Heights*:

> is often deeply inhospitable in the book, not easily subdued to human purpose, comfort or design. Landscape is thus never simply a setting or something to be contemplated in Brontë's work, but an active and shaping presence in the lives of its characters.

> [www.bl.uk/romantics-and-victorians/articles/
> walking-the-landscape-of-wuthering-heights]

Rural landscape – as central as it to the book and to its characters' actions, moods and thoughts – is only one of the landscapes described by Emily. Domestic violence, addiction and mental illness reveal a social aspect integral to the industrial landscape that pervades the mill town that broods down the hill from the parsonage; they create both a social and a cultural landscape, separate from but dependant on, the rural. And this, when viewed along with those glowering moors, only adds to the overall oppressive nature of the book's hinterland and influences how the characters behave.

Indeed, some of the contemporary reviewers picked up on this outrageous fusion. *The Examiner* believed the characters to be less civilised than the pre-bronze age Mycenaean Greeks: 'the people who make up the drama, which is tragic enough in its consequences, are savages ruder than those who lived before the days of Homer'. The *New Monthly Magazine* was equally appalled: the novel 'should have been called Withering Heights, for anything from which the mind and body would more instinctively shrink, than the mansion and its tenants, cannot be easily imagined … a perfect misanthropist's heaven'.

The book, then, its landscapes, its apparently rude middle class characters and their servants with their thick regional accents and the general 'grim up northness' – all this conspired to disturb the middle class sensitivities of the 'down south' press and their readerships, enabling reviewers to resort to vapid stereotypes about life and people in the north of England.

But these reviewers, and others after them, miss the point entirely. Emily's aim was to challenge and disturb the comfortable and naïve assumptions about life and society that prevailed in environments and landscapes to be found in, for example, publishing houses in the capital and places like them. Charlotte defends the essential 'rustic' quality of Emily's work:

> [It is] rustic all through. It is moorish and wild and knotty as a root of heath. Nor was it natural that it should be otherwise; the author being herself a native and nursling of the moors. … Ellis Bell [Emily] did not describe as one who found pleasure in the prospect; her native hills were far more to her than a spectacle; they were what she lived in, and by, as much as the wild birds, their tenants, or as the heather, their produce. Her descriptions, then, of natural scenery, are what they should be, and all they should be.

The mystic quality, the desolation and the innate barrenness are palpable, as when, for example, Nelly flees Wuthering Heights,

> I bounded, leaped, and flew down the steep road [from Wuthering Heights]; then, quitting its windings, shot direct across the moor, rolling over banks, and wading through marshes: precipitating myself, in fact, towards the beacon-light of the Grange.

[Chapter 17]

The magical quality is there when the Cathy is sucked into a life of misery at the Heights, obsessed with Peniston Crags and its 'fairy cave' as described by Nelly:

> The abrupt descent of Penistone Crags particularly attracted her notice; especially when the setting sun shone on it and the topmost heights, and the whole extent of landscape besides lay in shadow. I explained that they were bare masses of stone, with hardly enough earth in their clefts to nourish a stunted tree.

[Chapter 18]

However, the reviews quoted above take no account of this description Emily gives of the moors on a warm, sunny day when Cathy and Linton muse on what constitutes the perfect heaven: the landscape is by no means unremittingly bleak; here, it is positively bucolic:

> He said the pleasantest manner of spending a hot July day was lying from morning till evening on a bank of heath in the middle of the moors, with the bees humming dreamily about among the bloom, and the larks singing high up overhead, and the blue sky and bright sun shining steadily and cloudlessly. That was his most perfect idea of heaven's happiness: mine was rocking in a rustling green tree, with a west wind blowing, and bright white clouds flitting rapidly above; and not only larks, but throstles, and blackbirds, and linnets, and cuckoos pouring out music on every side, and the moors seen at a distance, broken into cool dusky dells; but close by great swells of long grass undulating in waves to the breeze; and woods and sounding water, and the whole world awake and wild with joy. He wanted all to lie in an ecstasy of peace; I wanted all to sparkle and dance in a glorious jubilee.

Anne Brontë (1820–1849)

Anne's unhappy times at Blake Hall near Mirfield where she worked as a governess for the Ingham family in 1839 are vividly recalled in *Agnes Grey* (1847). The moors around Haworth are referenced in the opening paragraphs: 'What happy hours Mary [Agnes' sister] and I have past, while sitting at our work by the fire, or wandering on the heath-clad hills'. We readers sense the homesickness and uplifting memories again in a poem in which Anne's feelings are vocalised by an orphan girl in *Verses by Lady Geralda* (1836)

> Why, when I hear the stormy breath
> Of the wild winter wind
> Rushing o'er the mountain heath,
> Does sadness fill my mind?
>
> For long ago I loved to lie
> Upon the pathless moor,
> And hear the wild wind rushing by
> With never ceasing roar;
>
> Its sound was music then to me;
> Its wild and lofty voice
> Made my heart beat exultingly
> And my whole soul rejoice.

The Governess, (1851) Rebecca Solomon (1832–1886). Blue pencil.svg wikidata:Q2508786
The governess wears black clothes and is occupied in teaching her pupil, while the probable daughter of the family that employs her is wearing a bright-coloured dress, and is musically flirting with an eligible man. The governess is aware that most young adult men of the genteel classes will almost completely ignore her socially (while a few will make crude sexual passes at her if they find her alone).

In *The Tenant of Wildfell Hall* Anne takes up the controversial themes and the social and cultural landscapes that had offended so many in Emily's *Wuthering Heights*: violence, inebriation and conflict are laid bare, based on the alarming and shabby treatment she received at Blake Hall, and on Branwell, her dissolute brother. Some scholars believe that Wildfell Hall is based on Ponden Hall, a farmhouse near Stanbury in West Yorkshire.

Anne Brontë's grave in Scarborough. © Mark Davis

Writing Haworth out of the picture

Moorland there is aplenty but, curiously, Haworth itself is conspicuous by its absence in the work of the three sisters: the petulant 'no other landscape than a monotonous street' description apart, the village rarely features. There is this in Charlotte's early poetry:

> when the crystal icicles are hanging from the eaves of the houses and the bushy evergreens are all spangled with snow flakes as if twas spring & they were flourishing in full blossom – when all the old women traverse the streets in great woollen cloaks & clacking iron pattons.

But this is more weather than Haworth; there is a satirical description of Haworth and the Brontës as the Howards in her *Angria and the Angrians,* and Anne's opening lines to *Agnes Grey* and Emily's homesickness expressed in

> The mute bird sitting on the stone,
> The dank moss dripping from the wall,
> The garden-walk with weeds o'ergrown,
> I love them – how I love them all.

(17–20)

This follows Emily's description of the cosy parsonage – in stark contrast to the wild moors outside, showing her to be a hearth-loving, but not necessarily a Haworth-loving, girl:

> There is a spot, 'mid barren hills,
> Where winter howls, and driving rain;
> But, if the dreary tempest chills,
> There is a light that warms again.
>
> The house is old, the trees are bare,
> Moonless above bends twilight's dome;
> But what on earth is half so dear–
> So longed for--as the hearth of home?

(9–16)
[Emily Brontë, A Little While, A Little While]

Indeed, being away from Haworth made Emily ill, and it was not just homesickness. Charlotte speaks of Emily's low mood when they were at Roe Head School near Dewsbury. Her pallid face, loss of weight and weakness compelled Charlotte to get Emily back to the 'dear … hearth of home'. Haworth itself clearly has none of the enveloping influence the surrounding moors had on the prose and poetry of the Brontë sisters. Perhaps it is because Haworth for the girls spoke of death: the premature death of Maria and Elizabeth, the early death of their mother, the overfull noxious graveyard with its legions of tombstones standing sentinel outside their windows, almost encroaching on their parsonage, and the frequent funerals keeping it overstocked. The girls would not have been aware of the statistic but, as noted, the average life expectancy in Haworth at the time was 25.8, no better than London or impossibly polluted Bradford down the road. For those who survived infancy life expectancy was around forty-four. Because of their father's efforts in relation to the sanitation issues, they may, though, have been all too aware that the sinister rains from the moors were incessantly trickling through the burial ground into the village water supply, ever replenishing the business for the local funeral services.

To exorcise Haworth's associations with death and the funereal, the sisters had to take themselves and their creativity to another place: the surrounding moorland provided a liberating, life affirming and vivifying landscape where they could run free, where the becks ran clear and where their imaginations ran riot. Unlike their situation down in Haworth, they were in control of their demons up on the moors, unleashing their own literary take on death, duplicity and destruction, notably in *Wuthering Heights*, *The Tenant of Wildfell Hall* and *Jane Eyre*.

Top Withens

Top Withens (SD981353) is a dilapidated farmhouse near Haworth that is reputed to have been the inspiration for the Earnshaw family house, Wuthering Heights, in Emily Brontë's novel of the same name.

Wuthering Heights? Not really. © Mark Davis

A helpful plaque on a wall tells us:

> This farmhouse has been associated with 'Wuthering Heights', the Earnshaw home in Emily Brontë's novel. The buildings, even when complete, bore no resemblance to the house she described, but the situation may have been in her mind when she wrote of the moorland setting of the Heights.
>
> [*Brontë Society 1964. This plaque has been placed here in response to many enquiries.*]

So popular are the Brontës with Japanese tourists that some footpath signs in the area bear directions in Japanese.

Other nearby sites include Brontë Falls, the Brontë Bridge, and the Brontë Stone Chair in which the sisters reputedly took turns to sit and write their first stories. There is also Ponden Hall nearby, believed to be the house called Thrushcross Grange in *Wuthering Heights*.

Ponden Reservoir on Haworth Moor in 2010. © Mark Davis

HAWORTH IN THE EARLY TWENTY-FIRST CENTURY

As we have already said, the Brontës inhabit and occupy the lion's share of modern life in Haworth: the Parsonage Museum – and its guardians, the Brontë Society – constitute a veritable magnet for anyone anywhere with an interest in our literary heritage, and for aficionados and researchers of nineteenth-century English literature and the nineteenth century novel in particular. The works of the Brontës also shed welcome light on the place of women in nineteenth-century society, on local West Yorkshire history, particularly as it relates to local industry, and on the relationship between landscape and literature.

As an example of conservation, the Parsonage Museum is compelling, faithfully conserving, informing as it does the world of the Brontës. But conservation in Haworth goes much further than the parsonage. Haworth is a conservation area that can boast over eighty listed buildings and many more that add much to the village's character. According to the Historic England website:

> Haworth has a chaotic but cohesive charm; buildings of different size, type and age are set at different angles and distances from the street, but are nevertheless united by their level of preservation and by the colour of the stone from which they are built. Together they reflect the gradual and organic development and the diverse assortment of facilities, employers, people and institutions once found in an industrious, self-sufficient Pennine hill village. They also provide the very fabric of the present-day living village, which is home to a thriving community and is also a popular and friendly tourist destination … The aim is to protect and enhance Haworth, and its international reputation as a high-quality tourist destination, for generations to come.

Add to this the Keighley and Worth Valley Railway, the Brontë-inflected moorland walks, the wonderful range of local shops, restaurants and pubs then you get a delightful Haworth that must continue to be conserved at all costs.

Here are just a few of the salient features of the village and its environs today.

The Wyedean Weaving Company is one of Haworth's major industrial companies and employers. It came to Haworth in 1964 as a manufacturer of 'narrow fabrics, braid and uniform accoutrement'. The business started in Coventry around 1850 when it was known as Dalton, Barton and Co. Ltd. During the First World War, the factory in Coventry was totally destroyed during the Blitz in 1941. The same fate befell the company's East End warehouse and store in Jewin Street, London. Company records from this time and before are, therefore, hard to come by.

Wyedean products on parade. Courtesy of MOD.

The Wyedean website reveals that the company:

> was formally founded on 7th April, 1964, by David Wright. Before starting his own business, David's first job after leaving school was as an apprentice textile designer at Bridgehouse mill. Little did he know that 34 years later he would purchase the very same building. In 1964, David bought from Dalton Barton the military side of the business manufacturing narrow fabrics and military ceremonial products. This decision started the process of turning Wyedean Weaving into the business it is today. He set out purchasing the appropriate machinery and moving the business to Haworth.

Wyedean today. Courtesy of Wydean.

122

Bridgehouse Mill as it was. Courtesy of Wydean.

The Old Silent, Stanbury

The way to the Silent Inn. © Mark Davis

The Brontës are not the only literary legends to exploit the area in and around Haworth. Martha Grimes, the best-selling US author of twenty-four mystery novels named after pubs – including 1989's The Old Silent, a moor-side pub at Stanbury less than two miles west of Haworth. This fine old stone inn dates back to the seventeenth century, with its unusual name first being mentioned in a 1908 novel by Halliwell Sutcliffe, *Ricroft of Withins*: 'Never, surely, was a hostelry so grim of visage, and yet so kindly of welcome, as the Silent Inn'.

Sutcliffe was born in Shipley in 1870 and died in Linton-in-Craven in 1932; he was an author of popular novels, most of them are historical romances set in the Yorkshire Dales. *Ricroft* was one of thirty novels in which Haworth is renamed Marshcotes.

123

The pub's name derives from the fact that Bonnie Prince Charlie hid there on his retreat from Derbyshire and the locals kept a life-saving silence for two weeks so that he could make good his escape. The pub website gives some lurid detail:

> Starting life as the New Inn and then changing to the Eagle Inn and eventually to the present name of The Old Silent Inn. Although the Inn dates back over 400 years earliest records show the premises to have been a family farming business in 1822   It is said that Bonnie Prince Charlie used the Inn as a hideout after he fled from Derby. The young Prince stayed at the inn for several weeks, relying on the silence of the locals for his safety and freedom. The villagers were told to 'keep silent' even under the threat of having their tongues cut out, there was also a 30,000 guinea reward (equivalent to about a £1,000,000 in today's money) placed on his head. Eventually someone told on him and the soldiers came down the hill from Stanbury to capture him. The Wishing Well restaurant at that time was a stable and Bonnie Prince Charlie's horse was always saddled up ready to go. When the soldiers were spotted his comrades went out to stop them, Bonnie Prince Charlie jumped on his horse and made haste towards Lancashire … In recognition of the act of the villagers keeping silent, the Inn was renamed The Old Silent Inn hence the present name.

[www. http://oldsilentinnhaworth.co.uk/about-traditional-pub/]

The publisher's (Little, Brown of Boston) website describes the Martha Grimes book:

> Richard Jury, the New Scotland Yard superintendent witnesses a killing in a West Yorkshire inn called the Old Silent, while his highborn, amateur colleague, Melrose Plant wishes he could perform one as he drives his impossible Aunt Agatha to the Old Swan in Harrogate.
>
> Caught up in a triple murder, Jury would go to any lengths to help Nell Healey, the lovely widow of one of the victims. But Nell Healey remains silent as the Yorkshire moors, quiet as the grave, while the scope of the mystery widens.

[www.marthagrimes.com/books/the-old-silent/.
Accessed 19 February 2018]

AROUND HAWORTH

Crosshills

Leeshaw Reservoir

The 1911 drought.

Cross Roads cum Lees

Bingley Road, about 1900.

Lees about 1900.

Oakworth

Oakworth House.

An Oakworth tea party.

Sykes Head, Oakworth.

Oxenhope

Uxenhope from Leeming 1900.

Oxenhope station and Gledhow from Hiram bridge.

Muffin Corner and Rose Bank house 1910.

Silsden

Bolton Road.

The Conservative Club.

Kirkgate.

Stakes Beck.

Stanbury

Smith Bank.

The Eagle Inn.

TOURISM AND CULTURE

From spa to 'Scroggling the Holly'

Haworth is not just about the Brontës, but the Brontës, of course, take the lion's share of the tourists' attention and they are usually why people visit the village from all over the world. Emily, Ann and Charlotte apart there is a long heritage of cultural events here that has lasted until the present day.

What **Haworth Spa** lacked in the Harrogate brand of prestige and refinement, it certainly made up for in the opportunities it offered for wilderness bathing and cold baths – cold baths that were exactly that. The remains of the spa can today be found on a moorland swamp with derelict buildings that were once bathhouses. The resort appears on the 1852 OS-map (SE 0041 3513), where 'at least two springs of clear water trickle slowly from the wet slope above you into the boggy reeds', according to Paul Bennett in *The Northern Antiquarian*.

The real expert, however, is Martha Heaton who, in her *Recollections and History of Oxenhope,* provides some intriguing detail:

> For many years the first Sunday in May was a special day. It was known as Spa Sunday, for on this day people gathered up in the hills overlooking what is now Leeshaw Reservoir, here was a well, known as Spa Well, and the stream which now feeds the reservoir is known as Spa Beck. People came from Haworth, Oxenhope, Stanbury, and other villages sitting round the well, they sang songs, some bringing their musical instruments to accompany the singing. Children brought bottles with hard spanish in the bottom filling the bottle with water from the well, shaking it until all the spanish or liquorice had been dissolved. This mixture was known as 'Poppa Lol' and would be kept for weeks after a little sugar had been added, then it was used sparingly as medicine. The custom seems to have died out when Bradford Corporation took over the water and made Leeshaw Compensation Reservoir in 1875, though up to about 1930 two men from Haworth would wend their way to the spot on the moor, the first Sunday in May. The men were John Mitchell and Riley Sunderland, better known, in those days as 'Johnny o'Paul's' and 'Rile Sun'.

It was a great day for many people. The *Keighley News* of May 1867 mentioned it thus: 'A large assembly met on Spa Sunday on the moors about two miles from Haworth, and a party of musicians from Denholme performed sacred music'. This locality was often visited during the summer months by the Brontë family.'

Haworth had its **rushbearing ceremony**, an English festival from the Middle Ages in which rushes and other herbs and grasses were carried to the parish church in order to be strewn over the earthen floor to provide a sweet smelling, renewable covering for insulation. It was well established by Shakespeare's time but declined in the early nineteenth century, when stone flags became the norm. The churches allocated a particular day for their rushbearing and, by the sixteenth century, it was usual to ring the church bells and provide wine, ale and cakes for the rushbearers; some festivals put on mimes. If this account from the ceremony at Cawthorne near Barnsley from 1596 is typical, then everyone had a whale of a time:

> the people did arm and disguyse themselves some of them putting on womens aparrell, other some of them putting on longe haire & visardes, and others arminge them with the furnyture of souldiers, and being there thus armed and disguysed did that day goe from the Churche, and so went up and downe the towne showinge themselves.

And that occasionally included members of the clergy:

> Tristram Tyldedesly, the minister at Rufford and Marsden on Sundays and hollidaies hath danced emongst light and youthful companie both men and women at weddings, drynkings and rishbearings; and in his dancing and after wantonlye and dissolutely he kissed a mayd … whereat divers persons were offended and so sore grieved that there was weapons drawn and great dissenssion arose.

As with all similar entertainment, rushbearing was a magnet for such disreputable varlets as pedlars, cutpurses, pickpockets, and for harlots; heavy drinking was the order of the day.

Haworth's ceremony is a thing of the past but it still survives in places such as Lymm in Cheshire; Saddleworth; Sowerby Bridge; Ambleside, Great Musgrave, Grasmere and Warcop.

The flamboyant and evangelist curate, Mr Grimshaw, brought an end to the popular **horse racing** at Haworth, which attracted 'profligate people to Haworth, and brought a match to the combustible materials of the place' [Gaskell, p. 26]. His fervent praying brought the rains down on one meeting allowing health and safety to prevail thereafter. To Gaskell, though, things seemed to go from bad to worse: 'I fear there was a falling back into the wild rough heathen ways, from which [Grimshaw] had pulled them up'. Generally, family feuds persisted 'as an hereditary duty, and a great capability for drinking, without the head being affected, was considered as one of the manly virtues'. Sunday **football** (using stones?) against rival local teams brought in 'an influx of riotous strangers to fill the public-houses' making the more sober-minded residents yearn for another Mr Grimshaw.

Death, too, had a stake in the conviviality, through the **arvill**. This was when the sexton announced from the foot of the grave the venue for the arvill – the Black Bull, for example. Mourners would then repair to said hostelry for 'refreshments', originally laid on to 'refresh' those mourners who had come from afar to pay their last respects. In Haworth, the poorer people provided a kind of spice cake for everyone while the copious alcohol – including 'dog's nose', a potent cocktail of rum and ale – was paid for from a kitty in the middle to which each family contributed. Up to eighty people might attend some of these arvills, and inevitably, as Gaskell tells [p. 28], 'up-and-down fights' sometimes erupted with the usual 'pawsing' and 'gouging' and 'biting'. Funerals were not the only excuse for bacchanalia: weddings gave opportunity for foot races run by half-naked men, gambling and cock fighting had to conducted with excessive quantities of alcohol and even the departure of Patrick Brontë's predecessor was marked with widespread inebriation.

'Thump Sunday' was still going in 1879. This was a Sunday on which the churches would get together to hold an outdoor service. The tradition was then to visit one's friends and family and eat copious amounts of spiced or plum cake and cheese. It was also the day when it was permissible on this day to thump somebody who went into a pub and refused to pay for his drink or buy a round. **Haworth Tide** – held the first Sunday after 11 October – was the annual fete.

Haworth Gala Group at Cross Roads

You could be forgiven for thinking that Haworth's **'Scroggling the Holly'** is an event of similar antiquity. It happens in late November when brass bands and Morris men noisily lead a procession of children decked out in Victorian costume, as they follow the Holly Queen up the Main Street cobblestones to the church steps for a grand crowning ceremony. The Queen unlocks the church gates to draw the spirit of Christmas into Haworth and Father Christmas arrives on the scene bringing glad tidings to all. In fact it is decidedly modern event ingeniously dreamt up and organised by the Haworth Traders' Association (now the Haworth Village Association) to mark the beginning of Christmas celebrations in Haworth.

The inaugural **Haworth Arts Festival** was held in 2000, was repeated in 2001, and then ended ... only to be revived in 2005 as a community festival combining performing and visual arts and street performance. The festival later extended across the Worth Valley Haworth and has featured John Cooper Clarke and John Shuttleworth, or is that Graham Fellows?

Haworth Band is one of the oldest secular musical organisations in the area with records of a brass band at nearby Ponden as early as 1854 founded by John Heaton. The band played a gig in Haworth to mark the end of the Crimean War. 'Over the years the world of brass band music went from strength to strength, during which time the Haworth Band went with it', according to IBEW, the Archived Histories of Brass Bands.

The site goes in to tell us how it all started:

> One Christmas morning in the early 1860s, the much respected Mr Hartley Merrall, well known as a manufacturer at Springhead Mill and himself a keen musician, was on his way to Haworth Parish church when he met a party of these musicians out busking. Mr Merrall listened to their music and invited them to his house that evening. He was determined to have a brass band of his own with the result that shortly afterwards the Spring Head Band was formed. This was to be the forerunner of the Haworth Brass Band ... The band enjoyed immediate success and went on to win the first of many awards in Keighley, Skipton and Trawden and also at Crystal Palace in 1863 ... in 1970, the classic film 'The Railway Children' was made, featuring a brass band made up of members of the Haworth band.
>
> [www.ibew.org.uk/cach-hawo.htm, accessed 11 February 2018]

One night, returning late at 2.00 a.m. from a concert the band decided to march from the station to the Black Bull, playing as they went up the hill. There were concerns within the players lest they wake up the residents along the route so they all agreed to take off their boots and process in just their socks.

The band continues to play at local galas, fêtes, shows and other events throughout the summer.

The Germans come to Haworth before the First World War.

Biplane landed at Manny Wells Heights, October 13 1913.

Haworth cricket club was founded in 1863 by the enthusiastic Crawshaw Dugdale. Later, it was divided along sectarian lines with the Haworth Church team pre-eminent before the First World War.

Haworth Ukelele Group is just that – group of enthusiastic ukulele players playing at varying levels and in various musical styles. Currently, they meet in The Old White Lion Hotel in Haworth. Every year at the end of June, the group organises HUGE, Haworth Ukulele Group Extravaganza along with performances at a number of local events throughout the year.

HUG performing at HUGE 2015. Courtesy of Haworth Ukelele Group.

Another highly popular event is a **1940s weekend** when Haworth goes back in time and where locals and visitors alike don wartime attire and engage in a number of nostalgic events.

Wehrmacht officers take Haworth.   Forties fashion and fun.

The thriving black market.

The sixties, too, were not forgotten as this nostalgiafest clearly shows.

Haworth was blessed with two cinemas: the Hippodrome, which opened in 1913, and the Brontë in Brow followed in the 1920s. The inevitable bingo followed the closure of the Hippodrome; it then became the Bygone Days Museum and is now flats.

The Hippodrome in 1961 after its closure.

From 1971 to 1988, 25 and 27 Main Street was a stone, three-storey former handloom-weaver's residence, the home of Haworth Pottery where **Anne Shaw** made hand-thrown domestic stoneware pioneered by Bernard Leach in the arts and crafts tradition.

In 2002, Haworth gained Fairtrade village status; hence the twinning with Machu Picchu in Peru.

On 6 July 2014 the riders of the Tour de France sped through Haworth; here are Charlotte, Emily and Anne taking a breather. © Mark Davis

Here is the rest of the pack. © Mark Davis

HAWORTH, THE BRONTËS AND THE PERFORMING ARTS

Branwell, Anne and Emily were accomplished pianists – Charlotte was precluded because of her poor eyesight for fear that reading the music would strain her eyes further. Haworth was something of a Mecca for music with concerts occasionally held in their father's church, for example the time when on 20 July 1846 there was a concert of celebrated tenors. *The Leeds Intelligencer* newspaper reported that the church was 'crowded to suffocation', and also that taking pride of place in the church was the organiser, the Reverend Patrick Brontë who it noted was 'now totally blind'.

The Haworth Philharmonic Society first struck up in the 1780s offering a spectacular concert every year, as well as occasional more modest events. These concerts were often held in the function room of the Black Bull Inn at a time when the girls would have been allowed into the pub chaperoned by their Aunt Branwell; Patrick Brontë habitually left the place at 9 o'clock when he retired to bed.

The concerts were nothing if not loud, raucous, and highly enjoyable affairs if this report of the 1834 annual concert in the *Bradford Observer* is anything to go by:

> The Philharmonic Society in this place, held a concert in the Large Room of the Black Bull Inn, on Tuesday evening, April 1st. The songs, catches, and glees were well selected. Miss Parker sung with much sweetness, and was highly applauded. Mr. Parker was in fine voice, and sang with his usual effect. Mr. Clark sung several comic songs with much taste, and was often encored, particularly in the song of 'Miss Levi,' which kept the audience in continual laughter. The concert was very numerously and respectably attended, and the company went away highly gratified.

The most celebrated performer was the German violinist, G.F. Hoffman, who in the Sunday school in December 1842:

> astonished a numerous audience by his extraordinary abilities as a musician, especially by his performance on the violin cello, entitled 'The Farmyard' … all was performed with first rate ability.

The Haworth Choral Society flourished in the 1840s and 1850s. Patrick Brontë was particularly partial to oratorio 'and often attended concerts and other meetings of an elevating tendency, in the village, taking with him the members of his family'.

The fame brought by the Brontës has made the village into something of a star – on the screen and in popular music.

Haworth and Haworth railway station appear as settings for films and TV series, including *The Railway Children* starring Jenny Agutter; *Yanks* (1979) starring Richard Gere and Vanessa Redgrave; Alan Parker's film version of Pink Floyd's *The Wall* with Bob Geldof; *Jude* (1996); *Brideshead Revisited* (2007), Vera Brittain's *Testament of Youth* (2015) and the 2016 film *Swallows and Amazons*.

Most famously, perhaps, is Edith Nesbit's 1906 novel of children having fun along a railway line, adapted into *The Railway Children*. It is largely shot in the Yorkshire Dales, but the producers needed a heritage railway, and the one that goes through Haworth was the only one in the UK in 1969 that could boast a tunnel, Mytholmes Tunnel. Director Lionel Jeffries grounded Jenny Agutter and Sally Thomsett when he caught them in a nightclub in Leeds after they had sloped off the set for a night on the town. The parsonage was used as the home of Dr Forrest.

Television programmes made at the KWVR include *The Great Train Robbery* (2013 BBC); *Spanish Flu – The Forgotten Fallen* (2009, Hardy Picures); *The League of Gentlemen* (BBC); *Last of the Summer Wine* (BBC); *Housewife 49* (2006, Granada Television); *A Touch of Frost* (ITV Productions); *The Royal* (YTV); *Some Mothers Do 'Ave 'Em* (BBC); *Born & Bred* (BBC); *The Way We Live Now* (2001); *Sons & Lovers* (2003); *North & South* (2004)and *Peaky Blinders*.

In 2016 the BBC drama *To Walk Invisible,* directed by Sally Wainwright, was shot in and around Haworth and included a full-scale replica of the Brontë Parsonage, Old School Rooms and Haworth Church on the moors in Penistone Hill Country Park, west of Haworth. Other scenes were shot in The Falcon Tap, in York's Micklegate.

It focuses on the relationship between the three sisters and Branwell in the last three dissolute years of his life. The title comes from a letter that Charlotte Brontë had written to her publisher about once meeting a clergyman who did not realise that she was actually Currer Bell. Their anonymity suited the sisters; after all, 'What author would be without the advantage of being able to walk invisible?'

Haworth gets back to 2016 after filming. 'And Chocolate', 54 Main Street, was a grocer's in the Brontës' day. The top photos were taken on the Tuesday, the lower that same Saturday. Photos courtesy of Simon Packham, 'And Chocolate', Haworth

Popular song

Most people are familiar with Kate Bush's Gothic rendition of ghostly Catherine Earnshaw's words, especially in the chorus – 'Heathcliff, it's me, I'm Cathy I've come home, I'm so cold. Let me in through your window' – and with Catherine's description of 'bad dreams in the night' as she pleads to be allowed in. Bush shares her birthday (30 July) with Emily Brontë.

Cathy running down that hill on Haworth Moor © Mark Davis

What is perhaps less well known is the reference to Emily, Anne and Charlotte by Kate and Anna McGarrigle in 'Love Over and Over' on their 1982 *Heartbeats Accelerating* album:

> You ask me how I feel I said my heart was like a wheel Why don't you listen to it sometime I've walked upon the moors On many misguided tours Where Emily, Anne and Charlotte Poured their hearts out And what did they know What could they know about love Or anyone know about love.

Literature

In Albert Camus' *The Rebel* (*L'Homme révolté*) Heathcliff is compared to a leader of the rebel forces. Both are driven by madness: one by misguided love, the other by oppression. Camus juxtaposes the concept of Heathcliff's reaction to Catherine with the reaction of a disenchanted rebel to the ideal he once held.

Sylvia Plath and Ted Hughes both wrote poems called *Wuthering Heights*.

There is no life higher than the grasstops
Or the hearts of sheep, and the wind
Pours by like destiny, bending
Everything in one direction.
I can feel it trying
To funnel my heat away.
If I pay the roots of the heather
Too close attention, they will invite me
To whiten my bones among them.

[Sylvia Plath, *Wuthering Heights*, 11–19]

It was the track for Stanbury. That climb
A mile beyond expectation, into
Emily's private Eden. The moor
Lifted and opened its dark flower
For you too. That was satisfactory.
Wilder, maybe, than ever Emily knew it.
With wet feet and nothing on her head
She trudged that climbing side towards friends
Probably. Dark redoubt
On the skyline above.

[Ted Hughes, *Wuthering Heights* 13–22]

Afghan novelist Khaled Hosseini's *The Kite Runner* references *Wuthering Heights* when Amir asks Soraya what book she is reading. Soraya replies, 'it is a sad story.'

Truman Capote's *Breakfast at Tiffany's*, has Holly Golightly bruise the narrator's feelings when she criticises his work and says he should aspire to the type of subject matter found in *Wuthering Heights*.

Yoko Ono's 'You're the One', from her 1984 *Milk and Honey* album compares Lennon and Ono's relationship viewed by society as similar to Laurel and Hardy, but viewed by the couple as Heathcliff and Catherine Earnshaw.

Jim Steinman's 'Total Eclipse of the Heart' was inspired by *Wuthering Heights*.

The title and cover of the 1976 album *Wind & Wuthering* by Genesis were inspired by *Wuthering Heights*. It also includes two instrumental pieces titled 'Unquiet Slumbers for the Sleepers ...' and '... In That Quiet Earth', respectively, which are the last words in the novel.

In an episode of *Monty Python's Flying Circus*, the troupe performs a sketch of *Wuthering Heights* in flag semaphore.

In the 1981 film *An American Werewolf in London*, two American tourists walking on the moors comment on hearing howling in the background that 'it could be Heathcliff looking for Catherine'.

In the 2002 Simpsons episode 'Helter Shelter', The Simpson family are all living as though it were 1895. Homer says that the children are all in bed, and asks Marge if he can 'wuther her heights'. She consents, but says that first she needs to remove her 'Victorian undergarments'. She blows out a candle, and then sounds are heard suggesting the underwear is made of metal.

Actor Johnny Depp was asked in an interview if he was romantic, and replied 'Am I a romantic? I've seen *Wuthering Heights* (1939) ten times. I'm a romantic.'

The Brontës are up there in the heavens in force. Charlottebrontë is the name of asteroid #39427; asteroids #39428 and #39429 are named Emilybrontë and Annebrontë respectively. The 60 km-diameter impact crater Brontë on Mercury is named in honour of the Brontë family.

February 2018. © Mark Davis

A HAWORTH–BRONTË TIMELINE

1066 Haworth not mentioned in the *Domesday Book*.

1545 population of Haworth ca. 300.

1660 population ca. 700.

1777 Patrick Brunty born in Emdale, County Down.

1779 The parsonage is built.

1783 Maria Branwell born in Penzance, Cornwall.

1790 Mills start to take over the cottage woollen industry. Population 3,164.

1802 Patrick, now known as Brontë, goes up to Cambridge.

1811 Luddism rife in Yorkshire.

1812 Now an ordained clergyman, Patrick meets and marries Maria.

April 1814 Maria Brontë, daughter of Patrick and Maria, born.

1815   Elizabeth Brontë born.

Patrick becomes curate at Thornton.

21 April 1816 Charlotte Brontë born.

26 June 1817 Patrick Branwell Brontë born.

30 July 1818 Emily Jane Brontë born.

17 January 1820 Anne Brontë born.

20 April 1820 Patrick becomes curate of Haworth; the family moves to Haworth.

1821.

15 September 1821 Maria Brontë (the children's mother) dies of ovarian cancer.

1824

A year after Patrick's spinster sister moved in with the family, Maria, Elizabeth, Charlotte and Emily are all sent to Clergy Daughters' School, Cowan Bridge, Lancashire (Lowood School in *Jane Eyre*).

1825

Maria and Elizabeth both fall ill at school and die at home

1831

Charlotte begins teaching at the Haworth Sunday school after completing her studies.

May 1832 Charlotte returns home.

1835 Branwell plans to attend the Royal Academy Schools in London, but the plan turns to dust.

July 1835 Charlotte becomes a teacher at Roe Head School; Emily becomes a student there.

September 1837 Emily becomes a teacher at Law Hill School.

1837

After years of producing unpublished work with Branwell, Emily and Anne, Charlotte sends her poems to Robert Southey, Poet Laureate, and tells him she wishes 'to be for ever known'. Branwell writes to Wordsworth.

December 1837 Charlotte and Anne return home after Anne becomes ill. Charlotte resigns her position.

1838 Branwell goes to Bradford to become a portrait painter.

March 1838 Emily returns home from Law Hill School.

April 1839 Anne becomes governess to the Ingham family.

December 1839 Anne is dismissed by the Ingham family.

May 1840 Anne becomes governess to the Robinson family.

1840 Charlotte sends part of a novel (Ashworth) to Harley Coleridge, who sends a discouraging reply.

August 1840 Branwell works as assistant clerk at Sowerby Bridge Railway Station.

February 1842 Charlotte and Emily go to Brussels as pupils at the Pensionnat Heger.

29 October 1842 Aunt Branwell dies.

November 1842 Charlotte and Emily return home.

January 1843 Charlotte returns to Brussels as a teacher in the Pensionnat Heger. Branwell becomes tutor to the Robinson family near York.

January 1844 Charlotte comes home.

June 11, 1845 Anne resigns from her position as governess to the Robinson family.

July 1845 Branwell is dismissed from the Robinson family, for having an affair with Mrs Robinson. His decline into alcoholism and depression begins.

1844–1845 Charlotte tries and fails to set up a school at Haworth Parsonage. Discovers Emily's recent poems and presses her sisters to publish a joint collection.

May 1846 The Brontë sisters' first book, *Poems*, is published, under the pseudonyms Currer Ellis and Acton Bell. Branwell and Patrick Brontë are not told about it. It sells only two copies in the first year.

1847 Publisher Thomas Newby accepts Emily's *Wuthering Heights* and Anne's *Agnes Grey*, but is slow to publish them. Meanwhile, Charlotte writes *Jane Eyre*, which becomes an immediate best-seller making 'Currer Bell' famous overnight. The three 'Bell Brothers' become subjects of fervent gossip.

19 October 1847 Charlotte's *Jane Eyre* published.

December 1847 Anne's *Agnes Grey* and Emily's *Wuthering Heights* published.

June 1848 Anne's *The Tenant of Wildfell Hall* published.

24 September 1848 Branwell dies of tuberculosis aggravated by alcohol and drug abuse.

19 December 1848 Emily dies of tuberculosis.

29 May 1849 Anne dies of tuberculosis.

1848 Charlotte reveals her true identity as a woman.

1849 Charlotte's *Shirley* is published. Charlotte, her husband and her father continue to live at the parsonage. Her second novel, *Shirley*, is published.

1850 Babbage Report signals the beginning of the end to the squalor in Haworth.

Charlotte contacts other famous writers to ease her grief. She keeps regular correspondence with Thackery, Elizabeth Gaskell and Harriet Martineau.

1853

Charlotte publishes her third novel, *Villette*.

1854

Charlotte marries Arthur Bell Nicholls on Thursday 29 June 1854.

March 31, 1855 Charlotte dies of tuberculosis and/or complications in pregnancy.

1857 Charlotte's *The Professor* is published.

Elizabeth Gaskell's *Life of Charlotte Brontë* ignites popular interest in the family.

1860 Yorkshire Penny Bank opened.

June 7, 1861 The Reverend Patrick Brontë dies aged 84. Arthur Nicholls returns to Ireland, and remarries three years later.

1867 Keighley and Worth Valley Railway opens.

1871 Census gives the population as 5,943.

1879 Currrent St Michael & All Angels' Church built between 1879 and 1881.

1893 Brontë Society formed.

1897 Co-op moves further down Main Street.

1906 Arthur Nicholls dies.

1925 Our Lady of Lourdes is the first Catholic church to open in Haworth.

1928 Sir James Roberts acquired the parsonage for £3,000, equipped it as a museum and gifted it to the Brontë Society.

Sheep on Haworth Moor. © Mark Davis

FURTHER READING

Adamson, A.H. (2008) *Mr Charlotte Brontë: The Life of Arthur Bell Nicholls*, McGill-Queen's University Press.

Alexander, C. (ed.) (2003) *The Oxford Companion to the Brontës*, Oxford.

Atkins, W.(2014) *The Moor: Lives, Landscape, Literature*, London.

Babbage, B.H. (1850) Public Health Act (11 & 12 Vict., cap. 63.) Report … on a preliminary inquiry into the sewerage, drainage, and supply of water, and the sanitary condition of the inhabitants of the hamlet of Haworth, London.

Barker, J. (2010) *The Brontës,* London.

Barker, J. (2016) *The Brontës: A Life in Letters*, London.

Barnard, R. (2013) 'Brontë, Patrick Branwell'. *A Brontë Encyclopedia,* Chichester, 53–57.

Barnett, D. (2017) 'Branwell Brontë: The mad, bad and dangerous brother of Charlotte, Emily and Anne', *The Independent,* 17 September 2017; on *We Need To Talk About Branwell,* with Simon Armitage and Adam Nagaitis, 7 October 2017 at the Parsonage Museum.

Baumber, M. (1977) *A Pennine Community on the Eve of the Industrial Revolution: Keighley and Haworth Between 1660 and 1740*, Keighley.

Baumber, M. (1983) *From Revival to Regency: A History of Haworth and Keighley 1740–1820*, Keighley.

Baumber, M. (2009) *A History of Haworth from Earliest Times*, Lancaster.

Bennett, P. (2009), Haworth Moor Spa Wells, West Yorkshire, Northern Antiquarian, https://megalithix.wordpress.com/2009/02/24/haworth-moor-spas/ accessed 11 Feb 2018.

Bentley, P. (1977) *Haworth of the Brontës*, T. Dalton.

Binney, M. (1979) *Satanic Mills: Industrial Architecture in the Pennines*, London.

Bowen, J. (2014) Walking the landscape of *Wuthering Heights*, www.bl.uk/romantics-and-victorians/articles/walking-the-landscape-of-wuthering-heights

Bradford Council, (2003) 'Haworth Conservation Area Assessment' (PDF). Appendix 2: List Descriptions of the Listed Buildings in Haworth Conservation Area: Bradford Council. April 2003. p. 32. Retrieved 13 February, 2018.

Birch, D. (ed.) (2009) *The Oxford Companion to English Literature 7th ed.,* Oxford.

Campbell, M. (2001) *The Strange World of the Brontës*, Wilmslow.

Chadwick, E.H. (2011) 'V. Haworth 1820–1824'. In *In the Footsteps of the Brontës*, Cambridge, p. 49.

'*Charlotte Brontë', Girls and their Ways. A Book for and about Girls by One who knows them*. London: John Hogg, 1881, 287–294.

Chrystal, P. (2014) *Old Saltaire and Shipley*, Catrine.

Chrystal, P. (2016) *The Place Names of Yorkshire – Cities, Towns, Villages, Hills, Rivers and Dales Some Pubs Too, in Praise of Yorkshire Ales*, Catrine.

Chrystal, P. (2017) *Old Yorkshire Country Life*, Catrine.

Chrystal, P. (2018) *Bradford at Work*, Stroud.

Chrystal, P. (2018) *Yorkshire Literary Landscapes*, Darlington

Chrystal, P. (in press) *Historic England: Bradford*, Stroud.

Cooke, W.H. 'A Winter-Day at Haworth' [1867], *Chambers's Journal* 217 (22 Feb. 1868), 124–128; and (1867–8) *St James's Magazine*.

Craven, J. (1907) *A Brontë Moorland Village and Its People: A History of Stanbury*, Keighley.

Daiches, D. (1979) *Literary Landscapes*, New York.

Davids, S. (1983) *Haworth in Times Past*, Newbury.

Davies, D. (1896) 'Haworth Thirty-Seven Years Ago', *Temple Bar and London Magazine for Town and Country Readers* 107, 132–139.

Davis, M. (2014) *Secret Bradford*, Stroud.

Davis, M. (2013) *In the Footsteps of the Brontës*, Stroud.

Davis, M. (2011) *Bradford Through Time*, Stroud.

Dews, D.C. (1981) *A History of Methodism in Haworth from 1774*, Haworth.

Dinsdale, A. (2013) *At Home with the Brontës: The History of Haworth Parsonage & Its Occupants*, Stroud.

Dinsdale, A. (2006) *The Brontës at Haworth*, London.

Drabble, M. (1997) *A Writer's Britain: Landscape in Literature*, London.

Du Maurier, D. (2006) *The Infernal World Of Branwell Brontë*, London.

Emsley, K. (1995) *Historic Haworth Today: An Illustrated Guide to the Historic Buildings and Families of Haworth, Stanbury, Oxenhope and the Worth Valley Railway*, Bradford.

Emsley, K. (1992) 'The Browns, Sextons of Haworth and their Families 1807–1876', *Brontë Society Transactions* 20, 296–303.

Emsley, K. (1991) 'The Chapelry at Haworth', *Brontë Society Transactions* 20, 162–169.

Emsley, K. (1990) 'The Manor of Haworth', *Brontë Society Transactions* 20, 35–38.

Feather, G. (1973) *Oxenhope: A Pennine Worsted Community in the mid 19th century*, Haworth.

Fraser, R. (1993) 'The Brontës.' In Marsh, K., *Writers and Their Homes*, London, p. 41.

Gardiner, J. (1992) *The World Within: The Brontës at Haworth: A Life in Letters, Diaries and Writings*, London.

Gaskell, E. (1857/1997) *The Life of Charlotte Brontë*, London.

Glen, H. (ed.) (2002) *The Cambridge Companion to the Brontës*, Cambridge.

Green, D. (2005) *The Letters of the Reverend Patrick Brontë*, Nonsuch Publishing.

Green, D. (2010) *Patrick Brontë: Father of Genius*, Stroud.

Greenwood, R. (2005) *Who Was Who in Haworth During the Brontë Era 1820–1861* (unpublished).

Hagan, S. (ed.) (2008) *The Brontës in the World of the Arts*, London.

Harrison, D.W. (2002) *The Brontës of Haworth: Yorkshire's Literary Giants: Their Lives, Works, Influences and Inspirations*, Bloomington, IND.

Heaton, H. (1965) *The Yorkshire Woollen and Worsted Industries*, Oxford.

Heaton, M. (2006) *Recollections and History of Oxenhope*, privately printed.

Hendrix, H. (2007) *Writers' Houses and the Making of Memory*, London.

Hewitt, P. (2004), *Brontë Country: Lives and Landscapes*, Stroud.

Hodgson, J. (1879) *Textile Manufacture and Other Industries in Keighley*.

Hüsken, W.N.M (1996) 'Rushbearing: a forgotten British custom.' In Johnston, A.F. *English Parish Drama*, Leiden.

Ingle, G. (1997) *Yorkshire Cotton 1780–1835*, Lancaster.

Jefferson, G (1969) *Libraries and Society*, Cambridge.

Jennings, H. (2012) *Pandemonium 1660–1886: The Coming of the Machine as Seen by Contemporary Observers*, London.

Jennings, M.A. (n.d.) *Transcription of the Grave Stones in the Church Yard of the Parish Church of St Michael's and All Angels*, Haworth (unpublished).

Jowitt, J.A. (ed.) (1991) *Mechanization and Misery: The Bradford Woolcombers' Report of 1845*, Halifax.

Kellett, J. (1977) *Haworth Parsonage: Home of the Brontës*, Haworth.

Kidson, A. (2014) *Yorkshire People and Places: Prints and Drawings from the Harrogate Fine Art Collection*, Harrogate.

Knox, J.M. (1999) The Name Howarth, http://www.haworthassociation.org/Reunions/1999Reunion/1999-name_origin.htm

Lamonica, D. (2003) *We are Three Sisters: Self and Family in the Writing of the Brontës*, University of Missouri Press; Chapter 6: *The Professor* and *Shirley* – Industrial Pollution of Family Values and Relations.

Lemon, C. (1993) *A Centenary History of the Brontë Society*, Haworth.

Lemon, C. (1996) *Early Visitors to Haworth, from Ellen Nussey to Virginia Woolf*, Haworth.

Lock, J. (1979) *A Man of Sorrow: The Life, Letters, and Times of the Rev. Patrick Brontë*, Information Today.

Meeker, C. (1895) *Haworth: Home of the Brontës. Brontë Society Publications. Part II. 2nd. Edn.* [Repr. from the Cincinnati Times-Star, Feb. 14th. 1895.] Bradford: F. Treweek & Co., 1895.

Mitchell, W.R. (1987) *J.B. Priestley's Yorkshire*, Clapham.

Myers, A. (1995) *Myers' Literary Guide: The North East*, Manchester.

Newton. J. (1799) *Memoirs of the Life of the late Rev. William Grimshaw, A.B., Minister of Haworth, in the West Riding of the County of York*, London.

'On the Yorkshire Hills about Haworth'. *Temple Bar* XIX (1867), 428–432. [Repr. in *Every Saturday* (2 March 1867), 275–277.]

'OPQ' (1858) 'Brunnel Brontë: A Warning to Young Men', *The United Methodist Free Churches Magazine*, 522–524.

People's Magazine (1867) 'A Visit to Haworth', *People's Magazine: An Illustrated Miscellany for Family Reading* 22, 376–378.

Pollard, A. (1988) *The Landscape of the Brontës*, London.

Povey, R.O.T. (1970) *The History of the Keighley and Worth Valley Railway*, Keighley.

Priestley J.B. (1953) *The Other Place*, London.

Priestley, J.B. (1937) *English Journey*, London.

Putnam, A.J. (1864) A Visit at Haworth, *The Monthly Religious Magazine* 31, 41–46.

School Register of the Clergy Daughter's School (1825) reprinted in *Journal of Education* 366 (1900), 36.

Shackleton, I. (2003) The Merrall Family Dynasty, www.haworth-village.org.uk/history/work/merrall.asp. Accessed 19 February 2018.

Smith, M. (1995–2003) *The Letters of Charlotte Brontë: 3 vols*, Oxford.

Southwart, E. (1923) *Brontë Moors & Villages from Thornton to Haworth*, London.

Stuart, J. A. Erskine (1888) *The Brontë Country: Its Topography, Antiquities, and History*, London.

Stuart, J.A. Erskine (1892) *The Literary Shrines of Yorkshire: the Literary Pilgrim in the Dales*, London.

Tomlinson, J. (1865) 'Haworth, where the Brontës Lived', *Some interesting Yorkshire Scenes*, London, 116–154.

Turner, J.H. (1879) *Haworth, Past and Present: A History of Haworth, Stanbury and Oxenhope*, Brighouse: J. S. Jowett.

https://archive.org/stream/haworthpastprese00turniala/haworthpastprese00turniala_djvu.txt

'Visit to Haworth. 'The Brontë Family', *Littell's Living Age*, 59: 754 [3rd ser. III] (6 November 1858), 474–475. [Repr. from Scotsman (9 October 1858).]

Walford, L.B. (1890) 'The Home of Charlotte Brontë', *Longman's Magazine* XV: LXXXVII 306–313.

Whitehead, S.R. (2010) *Ashmount, Haworth, the biography of a Victorian Villa*, Haworth.

Whitehead, S.R. (2017) *The Brontës' Haworth: The Place and the People the Brontës Knew*, 2nd ed., Haworth.

Whitehead, S.R. (2017) *The Last Brontë: The intimate memoir of Arthur Bell Nicholls*, York.

Wilks, B. (1991) *The Illustrated Brontës of Haworth*, London.

Wilson, F. (2016). 'Sisters are doing it for themselves: the Brontës' Own Story', *The Times Saturday Review* p. 11.

Wolfe, T.F. 'Haworth and the Brontës' and 'Brontë Scenes in Brussels', *A Literary Pilgrimage Among the Haunts of Famous British Authors*. 8th ed. Philadelphia: J. B. Lippincott Co., 1897 [¹1895], 121–135, 207–225.

Wood, S. (2004) *Haworth: 'A strange, uncivilised little place'*, Stroud.

Wood, S. (2009) *Haworth Through Time*, Stroud.

Wood, S. (2009) *Oxenhope and Stanbury Through Time*, Stroud.

Wood, S. (2011) *Haworth, Oxenhope & Stanbury From Old Photographs Volume 1: Domestic & Social Life*, Stroud.

Wood, S. (2011) *Haworth, Oxenhope & Stanbury From Old Photographs Volume 2: Churches*, Stroud.

Wood, S. (2014) *Haworth, Oxenhope & Stanbury from Old Maps*, Stroud.

Wynne, D. (2018) 'Charlotte Brontë and the Politics of Cloth: The 'Vile Rumbling Mills' of Yorkshire', *Brontë Studies* 43.

WEBSITES

…and Chocolate of Haworth and Ripon (www.andchocolate.co.uk/)

The Black Bull (www.blackbullhaworth.com/index)

Brontë Country (www.Brontë-country.com)

Brontë Parsonage Museum (www.Brontë.org.uk/)

Destinworld (www.destinworld.co.uk/)

Haworth (www.haworth-village.co.uk)

Historic England and Haworth (https://historicengland.org.uk/images-books/publications/haworth-village-of-Brontës/)

Keighley and Worth Valley Railway (www.kwvr.co.uk/)

Mark Davis Photography (www.mark-davis-photography.com/yorkshire/haworth/)

The Old Apothecary (the-curiosity-society.myshopify.com/pages/gallery)

Paul Chrystal (www.paul.chrystal.com)

St Michael's & All Angels (www.haworthchurch.co.uk/)

Wyedean (www.wyedean.com)

APPENDIX 1

Minutes of Haworth Urban
District Council 1895 – 1900

These random minutes from council meetings over a five-year period shine a fascinating light on the workings of the Council and on the working life of Haworth. In these extracts we learn about noisy pigeons in the bedroom, the prevalence of childhood infectious diseases, sanitation calamities, gender neutral stop cocks and plague prevention measures – along with a whole host of other mundane, but fascinating, local issues.

5th March 1895

That the Clerk wait upon Mr Albert Holmes respecting his claim for damages caused by an explosion of gas in his house and inform him that the Board do not acknowledge any responsibility.

4th February 1896

That notices be put out in the Council's Sanitary District warning persons against placing solids of any description in the River Worth and offering a reward for information leading to a conviction of any person so offending.

2nd June 1896

That the plant of Pig Stye proposed to be built for Thomson Smith at Greenfield be approved.

That all persons in the Council's District who have removed or allowed to be removed house numbers from houses be given notice that unless the same be replaced forthwith legal proceedings will be instituted against them for so offending and that the notice further warns persons against removing house numbers in the future as legal proceedings will be instituted against offenders.

Posters be put up at the scavenging tip in West Lane warning people against tipping rubbish on the ground except where provided for.

7th July 1896

That the Council's offices at Mill Hey be connected with the National Telephone Exchange.

That the law Clerk draw up a petition to the Postmaster General asking for a wall box to be placed at the bottom of Main Street Haworth and for the box to be emptied for each dispatch from Haworth.

1st September 1896

That a street sweeping machine be purchased at an estimated cost of £35.

That the top gateway at the cemetery be widened sufficiently to admit a horse and cart.

6th October 1896

That posters be put out in the Council's District offering a reward of £2 to any person giving information leading to the conviction of any person damaging gas lamps in the said District.

3rd November 1896

That a snow plough be purchased and that the matter be left in the hands of Mr Sladden.

1st December 1896

That five tons of salt be ordered instead of the two tons passed at the last meeting.

1st September 1896

That the plan submitted by Haworth Industrial Co-operative Society limited of a wooden butcher's shop proposed to be built in Main Street be approved subject to signing the usual agreement.

1st June 1897

That in commemoration of her Majesty's Diamond Jubilee a grant of sixpence per head be allowed by the Council for all teachers and scholars on the books of the Sunday schools for tea or other enjoyment.

6th July 1897

That Mr Richard Scull of 21 Brow Road be given notice to abate nuisance caused by keeping pigeons in the bedroom of his house.

5th October 1897

That a urinal be erected at the top of Changegate at an estimated cost of 12 pound providing that satisfactory arrangements can be made with General Rawdon.

That the Clerk laid before the committee a circular letter from the Cyclists Touring Club drawing the attention of the local authority to the damage done to pneumatic tyres of cycles by thorns which have been left upon the Highways. If it is possible for the upkeep and trimming of the adjoining hedges also pointing out that the same are a source of great injury to sheep cattle and dogs.

1st June 1897

That all the Council's servants be granted a day's holiday on Jubilee Day or some other day to be arranged.

7th September 1897

That all stop cocks fixed to the Council's water mains in future be known by the name of Female Stop Taps.

That the old crane belonging to the council at Dimples quarry be sold to Mr George Sladden for £2.10.0.

5th July 1898

That the plan submitted by the Haworth School Board for new school at Lees be approved.

That the plan submitted by the Haworth Industrial Co-operative Society for the erection of a shoemakers shop behind Main Street be approved.

That the Public Libraries Act be adopted in the Council's District Provided the trustees of the Mechanics Institute are prepared to hand over the money and books offered by them to the Council when the foundation stone of the Public Library has been laid but that no rooms be rented and no building erected until an effort has been made by means of public subscriptions and by other means to raise the sum of £700 for the purpose of erecting a new building and providing new books.

3rd January 1899

That notice be given to Mr A Holmes under section 91 of the Public Health Act for depositing slaughter house refuse too near to a footpath in Church Fields and the highway in West Lane.

15th May 1899

It was unanimously resolved that a free supply of gas be given to the Tradesman's Gala Committee for the purpose of filling the balloon on the third day of June next.

And that permission be granted to the Haworth Brass Band to erect their Bandstand on the piece of land at the back of the gasworks on condition that they appoint men to keep the public outside.

7th November 1899

It was unanimously resolved that the Clerk write to the local Police Sergeant with regard to the obstruction of Mill Hey on Sunday evenings by the congregating thereupon of crowds of young men.

5th December 1899

That handbills respecting dry ashpits be printed and distributed to every house in the District.

1st May 1900

That the Clerk reply to the letter received from the County Authority respecting the proposed erection of a police station at Haworth stating that the council have no remarks to make and prefer to leave the matter entirely in the hands of the County Authority.

7th August 1900

That the following plans be approved:- Wood shop in Mytholmes Lane for Mr J W Naylor, subject to agreement. Hen and Pig Cote in Tulip Street for Mr Jas Rawling.

That the Clerk communicate with the medical practitioners in the District with respect to the order from the local government Board respecting Plague.

That a man be advertised for to take charge of the steam road roller his duties to be stated in the advertisement.

6th November 1900

That Mr Rennie Bolton be appointed driver of steam roller at 25/-per week subject to rules drawn up by the council surveyor.

4th December 1900

That the charge for the steam road roller when out on hire be fixed at 30/-per day inclusive of engine man's wages coal, oil etc.

APPENDIX 2

Haworth Local Board of Health 1881–1894

The Board of Health is also an intriguing source of local information with issues ranging from the disposal of solid slaughter house refuse, pig sty maintenance, and boiling offal in River Street to mortality and similar statistics, an officially ignored petition in favour of women's suffrage, ashpits and privies.

6th December 1881

That a notice be served upon John Holmes Butcher prohibiting him from turning solid slaughter house refuse into the main drain and that failing compliance with such notice his slaughter house licence be discontinued.

7th March 1882

The Clerk was instructed to call the attention of Messrs Knowles to a nuisance on their Sun Inn property caused by manure liquid and a corner of the property being used as a urinal.

4th July 1882

The Nuisance Inspector reported that Joseph Wood the Board's scavenger was neglecting his duties in not emptying privies and ash places when they needed it.

1st August 1882

That the Schoolmasters of the district be requested not to allow children from houses where measles is prevalent to attend school and that the board respect the high rate of mortality amongst Infants as shown by the Medical Officers' report for the past quarter.

2nd January 1883

That notice be served upon the occupiers of the Black Bull Inn for the abatement of a nuisance caused by their allowing the overflow from a liquid manure tank on their property to overflow and run into a drain at the back of property belonging to John Holmes and others.

6th March 1883

The Buildings and Nuisances Committee recommended that the Nuisance Inspector having reported 20 cases of diarrhoea he disinfect all drains and privies where the disease has prevailed, that he forward samples of water from the different suppliers in the district to the medical officer for analysis.

3rd July 1883

The Clerk read a form of petition in favour of women's suffrage which had been forwarded to him for adoption by the board. No motion on the matter was made.

The Clerk read a letter from Mr James Ackroyd complaining of a nuisance at the back of his premises caused by the scavenger leaving the contents of a privy on or near the road for 94 hours. The Nuisance Inspector reported that it was an oversight of the scavenger and that directly the matter was reported to him (the Inspector) he caused the refuse to be removed at the scavengers cost.

2nd October 1883

It was resolved unanimously that plans (now produced) of three privies and ashpit in North Street for Messrs Sugden Pickles and Hudson be approved.

That notices be served on Amos Fletcher James Dixon JW Walmsley and Jane Roper to abate nuisances on their respective premises arising from the keeping of pigs and that a notice be served on Simon Drake of Aire Street to abate the nuisance on his premises arising from the keeping of poultry in his cellar.

6th November 1883

That a charge of £11.1.0 be made against Mrs Betty Binns for the services of the Fire Brigade and Engine in extinguishing the fire which recently took place on her premises, and that a gas stove be provided for the Fire Brigade House.

2nd June 1885

Haworth Urban Sanitary District
Annual report of the Medical Officer of Health for the year 1884
Area, 1830 acres; rateable value (1884), £8,258
Inhabited Houses (1871), 656; (1881), 877; (1884), 930.
Population enumerated (1871), 2884; (1881), 3816; Estimated (1884), 4180.

Population – The population of this district at the census of 1871 was 2,884, and that of 1881 was 3,816, living in 877 houses. I have estimated it up to the middle of 1884 to be 4,180, living in 930 houses.

Births – The total births registered in this district during the year were 106 in number, 55 males and 51 females. This is an increase of 10 upon last year, and is equivalent to an annual birthrate of 25.3 per 1000. The natural increase to the population is 18.

Deaths – There were 88 deaths registered during the year, of which 45 were males of 43 females. This is an increase of 3 upon last year, and is equivalent to an annual death rate of 21.0 per 1000 living, and is for the third year in succession the highest general death-rate in the Combined District.

6th October 1885

It was resolved that notices be posted giving defaulters in gas rents 21 days in which to discharge their accounts before taking proceedings.

It was resolved that the Clerk make application to the magistrates for an order to commit Daniel Wiley and Martha Whitaker to prison for non-payment of rates they having no goods.

6th April 1886

Sewerage and Drainage – There is no complete sanitary system of sewerage in Haworth. The original drains both main sewers and branch drainage were constructed of rubble. These have been replaced in different parts of the town and at different times by a proper sanitary pipe mains, and in all new houses during the past 14 years the branch drains have been laid in pipes. The drains from some houses in Main Street, Change Gate, and Brow, do not empty into the mains, but discharge on to gardens and land at the back of the premises. The sewage is irrigated on to land at the out fall from Main Street which brings the sewage from the upper part of the town but the outfalls from Coldshaw and Stubbing Lane, Bridgehouse Lane, part of Main Street and Hall, Station Road and part of Brow, and Mill Hey; all discharge direct into the river.

Ages at Death – It will be seen from the above table that the rates are all considerably lower this year. The infant mortality, or proportion of deaths of children under one year to births, is 11.9 per cent. That for England and Wales this year it is 13.8. There is also a satisfactory decrease in the deaths of children under five years (26.8 per cent), which is lower than it has been since 1878. Of the total deaths, 20 were those of persons aged 60 years and upwards, or a percentage of 29.8.

Mean Age at Death – The mean age at death for 1885 was 35.7 (37.1 for males and 34.0 for females). This is lower than last year, when it was 36.0, and not so low as in 1883, when it was 34.7.

Whooping Cough was prevalent in Haworth in September, and caused one death in a child, aged four months, at Mill Hey. A case of diptheritic throat occurred in a man aged 38, at Coldshaw, in April. A stopped drain was found upon the premises, which caused the sewage to back on to the cellar floor.

Fever – One death was returned from Typhoid Fever in August, from Clarendon Road, Brow, in a woman aged 52. The disease appeared to have been imported from Ingrow.

Slaughter houses, Common Lodging-Houses, &c. – There are 3 registered slaughter houses, and one common Lodging-House in the district. These have been inspected with regularity by Mr Readman, and are fairly well-kept.

1st March 1887

The Medical Officers' report of the health of the Board's district for quarter ended 31st December, 1886 was read and considered very satisfactory, it showed that the deaths for the quarter had been 16, equivalent to an annual mortality of 14.9 per 1000 living, and the births 22 equivalent to an annual birth rate of 20.5 per 1000 of the population.

6th March 1888

That the two public wells in Well Street and Main Street respectively be cleaned out and that placards be posted in the vicinity warning people against throwing rubbish into them.

4th February 1890

That John Appleyard of Mount St be given notice to abate a nuisance caused by excreta being deposited on the surface of Mount St.

4th March 1890

That notices to abate nuisances be served upon James Hey of Duke Street nuisance caused by ashpit being uncovered, Edward Sutcliffe of Gaugers Croft nuisance caused by dilapidated privy in West Lane, Willis Howker, caused by uncovered Privy tank in Violent street and Ward Peacock nuisance caused by his emptying excreta down grate in Main Street.

7th October 1890

A new Wesleyan school proposed to be built on Station Road be respectively approved.

1st December 1891

That the law Clerk write Mrs Touse drawing her attention to the fact that she has exposed her son who is suffering from an attack of Scarlet Fever both before and after being warned by the Nuisance Inspector and that if the Board have further cause for complaint legal proceedings will be instituted against her.

6th September 1892

That 1000 handbills and 50 posters containing precautions for the prevention of Cholera be ordered and that the former distributed and that the latter be posted under the directions of the Nuisance Inspector.

5th December 1893

That the following persons be given notice that unless they keep the pigs and pigstyes belonging to them at the places respectively named in a satisfactory condition that the Board would give them further notice requiring them to remove the pigs and pigstyes forthwith viz:- Betty Hoyle in Sun Street; Nathan Wright in Ouse Street; James Shackleton in Minnie Street.

5th June 1894

That legal proceedings be instituted against Mr Abraham Roper to compel him to abate nuisance caused by smoke and stench arising from boiling offal in River Street and that he be given 14 days notice to pull down a chimney erected by him without first having obtained plans approved in connection with stable in River Street.